MY LIFE WITH IBM

LUIS A. LAMASSONNE

Protea Publishing
ATLANTA

Author's email: luis@lamassonne.com

First Edition in English – translated with revision from the Spanish of the first edition.

English version edited by Michele Lamassonne.
email: michele@lamassonne.com

Protea Publishing
Atlanta, Georgia, USA

email publisher: kaolink@msn.com
publisher website: www.proteapublishing.com

author web page: www.proteapublishing.com/ibm.htm

ISBN 188370765x soft cover
ISBN 1883707668 hardcover
Library of Congress No. 00-111601

ISBN 1883707749 soft cover (Spanish Edition)
Library of Congress No. 00-111597

Front cover:
With Mr. T. J. Watson, founder of IBM, in 1950

To my wife, Lucía, who has shared my life and who helped me write this book, and to my dear children who translated it into English.

TABLE OF CONTENTS

INTRODUCTION

My Life with IBM is a book that describes the story of the life of Luis A. Lamassonne from the perspective of his association with that great company, IBM. It is a narration of his life that is easy and enjoyable reading, which takes the reader through a memorable trip through situations, places and interesting anecdotes.

This book is a clear example of a concept that is not commonplace at this modern business age, which is that of the loyalty of an employee to his company. At the same time, it is a true example for today's business community of the true values that make up a great company.

It is also a legacy to the family, showing the author's deep ties to family values and the love and dedication to each of its members. It shows the different faces of a man's life; that of a husband, a father and a grandfather. A friend of friends and one that shows great respect for his fellow human beings.

It is a life testimony and the mark that a man has made, that invites us to live every moment of our lives with intensity, making the best of every situation that we go through.

CHAPTER ONE

IN ARGENTINA

I believe that once a man has prepared himself to face the world, he becomes useful to himself and to society when he starts a serious job.

When I turned 23 in 1933, my friend Juan Bordes introduced me to IBM of Argentina (International Business Machines), an American company with three divisions: One for weight scales, another for clocks to register employee work hours, and a third and most important, the division for its Hollerith machines, baring the name of their inventor.

The general manager of IBM Argentina was an American, Sydney Wharing. After my first interview, I was hired and started as a student in the Hollerith Division. I was paid a good salary to learn how to work and repair these difficult electromechanical machines that would read and write by using punch cards. They performed accounting functions and compiled statistics. This was my first and only serious job in my life that lasted 38 continuous years. From that moment it was my "IBM" family.

Our instructor, Mr. Manuel Eirea, had just arrived from Spain, after having done the same teaching job before the Spanish Civil War. (Years later, when the war was over in 1940, I was sent from Buenos Aires to Madrid to do the same job).

At that time, a unit of IBM equipment was made up of several machines and some of them weighed up to a ton.

They all had different functions and names: The Puncher, the Verifier, the Sorter, the Tabulator, the Reproducer, the Collator and the Multiplier. Nowadays, with the arrival of electronics, a small personal computer on your desk can do the same work as all of those machines put together - and a thousand times faster.

After completing my studies, my first assignment was to work with an important customer, the Accounting and Statistics Office of the Ministry of Finance of the City of La Plata. IBM did not sell its machines then, but leased them to its customers. This particular customer had in lease a very large group of machines.

The city of La Plata is the capital of the Province of Buenos Aires and is the world's most perfect city. It was planned out in paper and then constructed on a large track of flat and fertile land, 40 miles distance from the city of Buenos Aires. I lived in La Plata and rarely had to go to IBM's central offices in Buenos Aires. Every day I would go directly to our customers' offices, where I had my own desk and all the necessary material to keep the machines running smoothly and our customers satisfied. All of these services were included in the monthly rent each customer paid.

I had a very good relationship with all the customers' employees and frequently helped them in their jobs, especially when it involved setting up a new application. On one occasion, I invented a special device in the Type 3 Tabulator that would catch the cards that would fall once the Receptor was full. This invention saved them a great deal of time, since they wouldn't have to classify the cards again after printing up a report. In order to do this, I had to modify the electrical circuit of the machine. It was mandatory to inform the company when we invented a new device, not only because it altered the original electrical circuit, but because in the United States, awards were established for those whose inventions were approved.

A few years later, I was promoted to workshop Manager in Buenos Aires, where I had personnel helping me in my duties. The Chief Engineer was Mr. Enrique Ober. Benito Esmerode was in charge of the Service Bureau and Mr. James Ruth was the General Manager of IBM Argentina. My new responsibilities consisted of refurbishing used machines and keeping them in perfect working order.

Someone had informed me that an important customer in Buenos Aires needed the Reproducer to perforate cards in a continuous sequence, something our machine did not do. Since we had several Reproducers in the workshop to refurbish, I worked on inventing a device in one of them to do what our customer wanted, even though nobody had requested it from me. When I finished and tested the new device, I let Mr. Ober know. At the demonstration of my modified Reproducer for Mr. Ober, to my surprise there was present none other than Mr. Ruth, our general manager. He congratulated me and mentioned how much my invention would solve a lot of problems.

After a short while, Mr. Ruth proposed I be sent to Spain for a year as an instructor and to help in the reconstruction of the company, which had deteriorated during the Civil War, between 1936 and 1939. The idea was for me to do the same job Manuel Eirea did years before. Mr. Eirea was currently the general manager of IBM in Uruguay. However, conditions in Europe were quite different from when he was there. Europe was in war and Hitler had taken over half the continent. Additionally, I had a girl friend and we had plans to get married, although a wedding date had not yet been set.

I made a quick decision to go - I was 30 years old with an adventurous spirit. I was leaving the easy life behind and I knew I would miss it. In Spain, even the most basic things were lacking - things I was used to during all my youth. For example, succulent Argentine beef. But, IBM was like a large family to me, where mutual loyalty was entrenched between company and employee. They needed me in Spain and to Spain I went on March 30, 1940 in the luxurious Italian ship "Neptunia". Little did anyone know it was the ship's last trip, as it was sunk by the enemy on it's very next voyage!

The trip was very pleasant. Our first stop was in Montevideo, Uruguay, where I was met at the port by my friends Eirea and Silvestre, the two highest level employees of IBM in Uruguay. We spent a very nice day together in the beaches of Pocitos and Carrasco. At night, the ship sailed to Rio Grande Do Sul in Brazil and we arrived there the following day at 11:00 a.m. At 4:00 p.m. that afternoon, we left Rio Grande and headed to Santos, a magnificent natural port. As in all Brazil, almost all the population is black or an interracial mix between black and white. Santos has beautiful beaches and a mountain called Monte Serrat, where they have put up a casino and where there is a church that was erected 400 years ago. This was my first visit to a church in a foreign country and I gave thanks to God for all the blessings I had received. I returned to the ship and at 6:00 p.m. we departed towards Rio de Janeiro.

On Thursday, April 4, 1940 at 6:00 a.m. Rio de Janeiro could be seen at a distance and at 7:30 a.m. we entered its magnificent port, considered the most beautiful of the world. Mr. Aloy from the IBM family in Brazil was there to meet me; I say family because this is the only family that will be with me in this mission I have set out to do. They took me to meet Mr. Valentin Bousas, General Manager of IBM in Brazil and then they took me to visit the plant and the offices of the company. After having lunch, we went to visit Copacabana and all the beauties of the city, and came back on board the ship at sunset.

The following day we sailed towards the port of Bahia. As we headed north, the heat got more intense and our favorite pastime was sitting by the swimming pool. At night the "Grande Ballo" was in the program of activities. At 9:00 a.m. we arrived in Bahia and with Roberto Robles, a friend who was an Argentine Diplomat, we took a taxi to see the city. It has 365 churches (one for each day of the year) and has more than 30 convents, which are historic relics. We had lunch on board and in the afternoon went to the beach with Delia Martinez, a young Spanish girl who lived in Madrid.

Sunday, April 7 - At 10:00 a.m., while we headed towards Pernambuco, the Chaplain of the ship presided mass in the ballroom, which was an important event since the majority of the first class passengers were Catholic, including myself. In the afternoon they showed a good movie and at 8:00 p.m. we arrived in Pernambuco (Recife). I disembarked to mail several letters and I walked through some streets that were very modern and that had magnificent buildings. At midnight, we set sail from the last port of the Americas.

Since leaving South America we would no longer arrive at a port during seven days of sailing until we reached Las Palmas, the activities and entertainment on board were intensified in order to keep the passengers happy. At 10:00 a.m., when we crossed the Equator, in the presence of the Captain and of "Neptune", we received an Equatorial baptism in the swimming pool. At 4:00 p.m. we sailed alongside the Island of Fernando de Noronha and after dinner that night, the entertainers and artists on board presented a variety theater. After that, a Gala Ball to celebrate the crossing of the Equator, which lasted until sunrise.

Tuesday, April 9 - Several activities were organized by the crew for the passengers on board, because of the many days ahead that we would be at sea. Several tournaments took place such as swimming, bridge, golf, ping-pong, plate shooting, etc. Every afternoon there would be a good movie and then dancing in the evening.

Wednesday, April 10 - We started to note that the warm weather was decreasing while we got farther and farther from the Equator. Today there was a special meeting with all the passengers that were going to get off in Spain to give us some important news. Due to the European war, the ship would now not stop in Barcelona! Therefore, they would drop us off in Lisbon, the capital of Portugal, and from there we would take a train to our final destination, and the ship would go directly to Italy. That night, a fakir artist put on a great magic show.

The following morning, Thursday, it was cool and cloudy. In the afternoon we could see off in the distance the islands of Cabo Verde and we subsequently sailed between the islands and the African continent. A warplane flew several times over the ship and then disappeared. On Friday we also had cold weather, but clear skies. The chief of machinists of the "Neptunia" invited us to the machine room of the ship. It had four diesel motors that worked simultaneously and each one moved a propeller. Each motor had 4,700 horsepower and would consume 80 tons of fuel every 24 hours. This would keep the ship sailing at 20 knots. It also had four electric generators of 650 kilowatts each.

On Saturday, April 13 at midday we arrived in Las Palmas in the Canary Islands which is a free port, and since merchandise is tax-free, things were quite inexpensive. The ship refueled. Las Palmas is an old city, but picturesque. It is called the "Door to Spain" because of the many similarities it has with Spain. As evening came upon us, we boarded the ship and set sail. The following day we arrived near the city of Funchal, the capital of the Portuguese island of Madeira. We couldn't go to port because of the low waters. A small motor boat took the Martinez Carrera sisters, Alfredo Scarrone and me to port. Together we went up the mountain, on an ox-driven sled, which is the vehicle most common and most ancient of the region. The Portuguese call this land "o paraiso do Mundo" - paradise! We had some unexpected adventures here which delayed our return to the ship and when we got to port, to our dismay, the ship had left. We got on a speedboat, which reached our ship. The crew threw us some rope stairs and with the boat sailing towards Lisbon, we climbed aboard.

On Monday the 15th we again had another cloudy and cool day. I got up very late and went directly to have lunch, like most of the young people, since I had gone to bed at 5:00 a.m., as was the custom on board. We had a superb grand gala farewell party the night before, since most of us would be leaving and going our separate ways that Monday evening upon landing on European soil. During that last day of sailing, we saw many war ships of different nationalities sailing near us.

As planned, in the evening we landed in Lisbon and all of us who were to get off in Barcelona got off there. After filling out all of my immigration paperwork, I checked into the Bragansa Hotel on Alecrin Street. There I met up with Dr. Rafael Nuñez Pereira, who was also a passenger on the "Neptunia" and who knew the city very well. That night, he showed me Lisbon's nightlife.

On Wednesday April 17, Dr. Pereira and I went sightseeing all day long. Lisbon is also an old but very beautiful city. We went to "Los Jeronimos", a relic which dates back many centuries, and where you can see the tombs of important figures in Portugal's history: Camoens, the poet, and Vasco de Gama, the conqueror. We also visited the house where Saint Anthony of Padua was born. In the late afternoon I boarded the international train at Rossio station to Madrid, Spain. The train stopped for three full hours for customs and immigration procedures when we reached Valencia de Alcantara on the Spanish border.

At 9:30 a.m. on April 18th I arrived safe and sound in Madrid, a city where I was hoping, God permitting, I would spend part of my life.

CHAPTER TWO

IN SPAIN

When I was on board the "Neptunia" and my travel plans changed, I didn't worry about communicating to Madrid my change in plans. Therefore, there was nobody from the IBM family to greet me upon my arrival. I checked into the Hotel Capitol and thereafter I started looking for the offices of the "Watson" Company, which was the name of IBM in Spain. It was no longer located on Avenida Jose Antonio 16, but was now on Avenida Calvo Sotelo 4. There I met Mr. Ross, partner agent of the company; Mr. Fernando de Asua y Sejornant, the general manager and also a Spanish aristocrat, and the Assistant Manager, Mr. Llopis, who took me out to lunch that day to a very elegant restaurant. Since it was Thursday, there was only one menu selection, as was the custom in Spain at the time, due to the scarcity of provisions as a consequence of the last three years of civil war.

The following day, April 19, was the national holiday of Unification. All business and commerce was closed that day and there were great parades headed by General Franco with the "flechas" and "falange" and Guardia Mora. In the afternoon I went to the Boite Italica and in the evening to Gaviria. The next day which was Saturday, and which was a workday until 2:00 p.m., I was taken to visit our company's most important customers. In the afternoon I went to Chanmartin de la Rosa to visit the family of my friend Mena from Argentina. Then on Sunday afternoon, I went to see my first bull fight, invited by the Martinez Carrero family. My first personal impression was that it was a barbaric show, in the middle of a civilized country and viewed by 20,000 excited and passionate fans. Nonetheless, my ill impression of the spectacle died away when we went to Casablanca Cabaret to dance.

During my first stay in Madrid, whenever I would be there for a reasonable period of time, I would visit different people that were recommended to me by friends in Argentina, who also later became my friends. Among them, Carmen Gabucio Sanchez Marmol, by suggestion of my journalist friend, Guillermo Korn; The Perez Ortega family, by suggestion of Juan Chiarelo; Mr. & Mrs. Manuel Fernandez, and many others who made my stay in Madrid so pleasant and who I grew close to and who I will never forget. These new friends were witnesses, as was I, of the great tragedy that Madrid went through during the three years of civil war. They would take me by the hand to places such as the University City, which was still in ruins, or to the West Park, where there was constant combat.

One of the main reasons for my going to Spain was that our company's technical service to our customers was not good. Therefore, instead of starting the instructional course, I took hold of the Engineering Department and started to visit all of our customers who used our accounting and statistics equipment, in order to improve our service to them. The two most important customers were the MZA Railroad and the Spanish Telephone Company. But in Barcelona we also had important customers under the same conditions of bad service, so I had to do the same in that city too.

On May 10 at 9:30 a.m. I left Madrid to Barcelona by train from the Atocha Station. At three in the afternoon we passed by Zaragoza and during the whole train ride you could notice the great destruction caused by the civil war. At 11:00 p.m. I arrived in Barcelona, and I was met by the general manager of our offices, Mr. Miguel San Mateo. Since I was going to be staying for a long while in Barcelona, I was booked at the hotel near to the office, the Hotel Splendid in Calle Pelayo 8. The following day, Saturday morning, Miguel came to pick me up to visit one of our customers, Compañia de Riegos y Fuerza. As happened in my visits to customers in Madrid, we had to work hard in order to satisfy our customers with our service. In the afternoon we rode up on the sky-rail to Mount Tibidabo, where you could see a panoramic view of the city and the port and surroundings.

Ever since I arrived in Spain, I noticed that in this country there are many national and religious holidays. That Monday, May 13 was a religious holiday for the province of Cataluña, so I had the opportunity to make contact with the list of the friends of my Argentine friends. The first was Olegario Martrat, a very bright and aristocratic young man from Cataluña, more or less of my age. Olegario was born and raised in Barcelona and he introduced me to many of my future friends, which made my stay in Barcelona very pleasant. They would take me to historical landmarks, to concerts or to a place to have fun and to dance.

During these 68 days of my first stay in Barcelona, I really learned to put in practice the saying "work before play". I worked a lot but I also spent my free time to get to know this beautiful country. My new friends took me to the most important places: the old or "gothic" city, with artwork from Sert, especially the "chronicles" showing the invasion of Cataluña by the Turks and the cathedral where each stone has historic value or is the resting place of many famous people. Or they took me to savor their culture in the Liceo Theater, or out on a speedboat and from sea observe what I was not able to see when I arrived from America: the view of the magnificent port with the Montjuich Castle in the background and then disembark and go up in an elevator to the top of the Christopher Columbus bronze statue, which is 54 meters tall and weighs 250 tons.

In Barcelona I had an assistant - Corredor, a young technician who didn't know much, but who was willing to help, and with my help, learned to improve the service to our customers. Among them were the Catalan Gas Company, Comercial Vila and Pirelli. The manager of Spain came from Madrid to visit, Mr. Fernando de Asua, an aristocrat, very proper for the job. Although he didn't tell me this, he came to personally check out how I was performing in my duties, particularly my relations with the customers and the other employees in the Barcelona office. As always, he would stay at the Ritz, which is the best hotel in the city. We had lunch together and Miguel San Mateo joined us and the following day we accompanied him to Paseo de Gracia station, where he returned to Madrid.

Everything in this city was very different and interesting. In my work I had gotten to meet the most serious and hard-working businessmen of Spain. The Catalan race is very industrious and entrepreneurial. There are factories of all types, but particularly the textile industry is very strong. The textiles produced here are of the same quality as the English ones.

In 1929 Barcelona became famous for the World's Exposition. You can still see some of the buildings created for this event, such as the Grand Palace of Expositions and Pueblito Español, which is a reproduction of all the typical regions of Spain. But what most left an impression on me was going into the historical fort of Montjuich where the security guard let us in and showed us the Santa Elena Pit, famous for the executions carried out there during the Civil War. There is now a statue erected in the place where those horrific crimes took place. I was also very stirred by the Corpus procession on May 23. The city was all festive with flags and flowers, as they were trying to revive this holiday which was banned since before the Civil War.

I also enjoyed things that were new to me such as the "Canodromo de Piscinas y Deportes" on Sarriat Street. It is similar to our horse races, but with very fine dogs instead - 10 races in all. Six dogs to a race and there are mutual bets. There are also what they call "quinelas" with two competing dogs. The other thing that was new to me was "fronton de pelota vasca", a very popular sport in Spain, similar to squash or racquetball.

On weekends I went hiking with my friend Banchs and with other members of the Barcelona Hiking Club (Club Montañes de Barcelona - CMB). We would get up very early and catch the MZA train to the north. In an hour we would arrive to the town of Cardedeu, where we would get off and start our upward hike with our backpacks towards Montseny. In the Primavera campground we would set up camp, pitch our tents and light the campfires. We would eat dinner and then sit around the campfire and sing Catalan songs, always in the company of our very good and romantic girlfriends... The following day we would get up early with splendid weather and toward midday we would go swim at the reservoir that was used primarily for irrigation but that had very pure water filled by mountain streams. The countryside was beautifully laden with wild flowers, which appeared to be planted by man. At nightfall, we would head back and we would arrive back in Barcelona at midnight.

Other times with Banchs and other friends from the CMB we would get up at dawn, we would catch the train at the Plaza España that would take us to Monistrol. From there we would start our hike going up Santa Cecilia, until we arrived at the Montserrat Monastery, at a height of over 1,000 meters (3,200 feet) above sea level. We would visit that traditional temple and then we would continue our hike to the Collbato Caverns, which were abandoned. We would descend into the caverns with ropes and lanterns.

We wouldn't neglect our cultural and social life either. We would go frequently to the Liceo Theater or to the Palace of Music and to the weekly concerts in the "Oro del Rhin". We would also drink vermouth in the Lido Cabaret with our girlfriends and we would finish the night dancing in a famous and popular place, the "Casa Llibre" or in the Casa-blanca Cabaret.

Toward mid-June, the European war was reaching its high point. The Germans had already entered Paris. And here in Spain General Franco had signed a decree declaring his country "not at war". He ordered the Spanish troops that were in Morocco to move to Tanger with the objective of protecting the law and order in this international territory.

I spent a few days in the Balear Islands and after reviewing with Miguel San Mateo that our operations in Barcelona were running smoothly, I said good-bye to our important customers, such as Mr. Campbell of "Riegos y Fuerza", accompanied by San Mateo. On July 17 in the evening, San Mateo took me to the MZA train's main terminal and I bid Barcelona farewell, after living there for 68 days. I traveled in a comfortable sleeper coach to Madrid. I arrived in Madrid the following morning at 10:00 a.m. and that day was a national holiday of the "Alzamiento" (rebellion). I stayed at the Hotel Peñon on Velasquez 8, which was very close to the office.

The following day I went to the office in the morning to organize the instruction course that I was to start teaching the following Monday. Over the weekend I was with my friend Delia Martinez Carrero and we went to "Gaviria" and to the Retiro Park. We said our good-bye's as she was going to San Sebastian for a month's vacation with her sister.

Classes started on Monday, July 22. Mr. De Asua and Mr. Ross started with some brief words of introduction and at that point forward I was fully in charge of the course as the official instructor. Photographs were taken and after I spoke a few words requesting the cooperation of my students, I initiated classes. All of my students were young and with basic knowledge of engineering, but they all were very eager to learn.

To make the learning process for my students easier, I started writing an instruction book in Spanish, since the only thing that existed were pamphlets in English that came with each machine, and my students didn't know English. Every night, when class had finished, I would stay at the office and with the help of Gaspar Martinez, the secretary of the Company, we would work on my book. Martinez would type what I would dictate to him, and together we would look up technical words in the dictionary that would be translated into Spanish for the first time ever. It was hard work that I took upon myself with good spirits, and that was outside my obligations and that nobody had requested of me. This was the first book that I wrote in my life of which I still have the original and that was my gift to my students and to IBM of Spain.

Since in Madrid I also led my life working hard, having a good time and sleeping little, I got used to sleeping 4 hours every 24. This city was ideal for this schedule, since everything started very late in the evenings. Dinner was always after 10:00 p.m. and after 11:00 p.m. is when the shows, the movies, the dog races, evening dancing and the "fronton de pelota vasca" games would start up. The biggest fronton game was that of the "Recoletos" where big wagers would be made while the game played on.

I never mixed my social life with any of the members of the many IBM offices where I worked around the world. In Madrid I enjoyed the company of magnificent friends that I will never forget. Many were members of the Spanish nobility and others were professionals or artists. Many of them have already passed away, but their names will never be erased from my memory... Delia, Carmen and Victoria Martinez Carrero, Manuel Fernandez and his wife Carlota Rafecas, the Marquis of Ugena and all his large and distinguished De Oñate family. I was friends with all of his children, especially with Rosa Maria and Maravillas.

Maravillas got married with Jose Maria de Gullon, and one of their sons, Manuel, the Count of Tepa, is the "Gentilhombre" of the Pope in Rome for the regions of Castilla and Leon, in the Order of the Holy Sepulcher of Jerusalem.

Now, when I am writing these memoirs at 87 years of age, I want to dedicate a few short words to "Manolo" (Manuel). When he finished his last year of high school in

24

Madrid, his father sent him to my house in New York in order for him to improve his English. He took part in everything that my children did, not only by living with us but by also going to the same school, and thus I consider him like a son. Since Manolo is a direct descendent of the famous Spanish conquistador, Juan de Oñate, who 400 years ago colonized the states of Texas, New Mexico and Arizona and who introduced the first horse to the United States of America, he has been invited by the Governor of Texas, George W. Bush, to celebrate this event which will take place on April 28, 1998 (next year).

Among other events, they will unveil a statue of Oñate on horseback. It will be in bronze and will measure 11.5 meters in height, which will be the biggest bronze statue ever made in the United States. The face of Oñate is that of Manolo and the sculptor made a trip to Madrid exclusively to use Manolo as the model. There will be a large military parade in El Paso, Texas, which will be a big event. God willing, I will be accompanying Manolo for the festivities. Another fraternal tie that I have with Manolo is that I too belong to the Order of the Holy Sepulcher of Jerusalem in the grade of knight commander.

And now continuing with my life in Madrid, my work was coming along well and I would do it independently and enjoying it too. I got a small apartment in Independence Plaza 8, in the Puerta de Alcala. My bedroom window had the view of the Retiro Park. Aside from it being a very nice place, it was also very conveniently located 3 blocks from the office.

In my free time I made it a point to get to know Spain and its historic places, which I had read of as a child when I learned history and geography of "the mother country".

Therefore, when I visited those places I would feel spiritually connected.... See and touch the Escorial, its Monastery and the Prince's House; Or Toledo with its Cathedral, its castle and the Greco Museum, with the famous work of art "the Funeral of the Count of Orgaz"...

During the months of July and August it is very hot in Madrid and most people would leave the city to go on vacations. The favorite vacation spots were the country farms or the beaches, and the San Sebastian beaches were the preferred ones. At the end of August, before the summer season ended, I decided to spend a few days in San Sebastian where my friends Martinez Carrero were spending the summer. I stayed at the Hotel Avenida, the same one where my friends were staying at. They had a nice set up with a canopy in the Ondarreta beach, which is smaller than the most popular beach of La Concha where most people go. We would go to the beach every morning and in the afternoon we would visit around. In the evenings we would dance either at the Tennis Club near Mount Igueldo or at the Club Nautico.

One Sunday afternoon we went with the Marquis of Monterron to the Lasarte horse races, where the most important horse race of the season was going to unfold. There was representation from the horses of the Count of Romanones and from the Marquis of San Damian. Obviously, all the Spanish Nobility was present and most of the European Nobility too, since this was the only oasis in Europe without war.

And speaking of war, one afternoon we went to Irun with some French friends, who were left speechless and crying when we arrived to the French border near the Bidasoa River and they saw Hitler's flag flying instead of the beautiful French flag. Only a few days before the German troops

26

had occupied all the south of France. From the shore, next to the Spanish flag, you could read the following inscription: "Year 1936 - the 5th of September" "Occupation of Irun by the Navarros". "Citizen: see the flag, symbol of the Great Spain. Welcome if you have not forgotten it, and do not enter if you offended it."

I really liked San Sebastian. It was obviously the beach in vogue where the beautiful people of Spain would go to in the summer. I remember that King Alfonso XIII would drive his car from Madrid to San Sebastian and would establish his office in this city in the summer during the last years of his reign. In the first days of September I returned to Madrid in the night train "Sud Express". My new friends gave me a going away party and Delia Martinez and the Marquis of Monterron took me to the train station. So many people were returning to Madrid that night the train was packed to full capacity. Even though the sleeper coach is quite comfortable, I didn't sleep well that night and I arrived in Madrid at 11:00 a.m. - half an hour behind schedule. Due to the war there was a shortage of gasoline and in the northern train station there were no cabs. Government authorities had organized a bus service that took us to our respective homes. I arrived somewhat sick and feverish and I went to bed.

Not feeling quite myself, I went to my office anyway the following morning with a stiff neck. Since I still had a fever, Fernando de Asua told me to go back home and sent a doctor to see me the following day, Dr. Becerro Bengoa, who prescribed an ointment, some pills and rest in bed. The doctor would come to visit me every day, but since the fever kept getting worse, after the third day he had me get up and go to his office so that he could run a series of tests and do a thorough exam. After that, he recommended I see a specialist. Asua took me to Dr. Avial, a friend of his and a gastro-enterologist, who after not finding anything abnormal, sent me to another specialist, Dr. Castañon, who from that point forward became my personal doctor.

Dr. Castañon made several x-rays and blood tests and he ordered rest in bed. While Dr. Sanz Extremera finished up the clinical tests, Dr. Castañon prescribed some injections of "Zeltia", a liver extract, and a nurse would come every day to apply the injections. After many days of uncertainty as to what I had, finally the professionals realized what it was. Dr. Castañon came to the house to tell me what I had: Para-typhoid A fever. He therefore prescribed "Piramidon" injections, absolute rest in bed and a diet of dairy products, eggs and white fish.

Every day Dr. Castañon would come and visit. He brought a graph to make note of the daily statistics of my fever and pulse, as is done in hospitals. He calmed me down by telling me that what I had was milder than typhoid fever, but that I would need to be in bed many days, since the fever at this point was still going to get higher. I was very depressed, since this was the first time I had ever been seriously sick in my life and I was alone in another country. But here is when I was convinced that there was an "IBM Family" all around the world. My friends, Asua and Llopis, who were the highest ranking employees of the company in Spain, were my family who would visit me every day and had at my disposal all sorts of things to comfort me, including feeding me a special diet every day during this long illness. Since there was no such thing as television, they brought a radio and many books to entertain me.

After being in bed for a whole month, Dr. Castañon,

who as I said before would come and visit me every day at 6:00 p.m., told me that the fever had disappeared completely and that I could get up and start walking little by little. I must confess that I had to learn to walk again. I had lost a lot of weight and I would lose my balance. After practicing and taking small steps at home, on a beautiful fall day in mid-October, I adventured out and crossed the street into the Retiro Park. Exhausted, I sat down on one of the benches, and looking up at the sky, I thanked God for having returned me to good health... Afterwards I learned where I had gotten the Typhoid fever from. There were two aqueducts in Madrid and one of them had been almost totally destroyed during the Civil War; This is the one that provided water to the area where I lived and it was recommended not to drink this water, but I did not know this...

I quickly started feeling better and started going back to the office. I worked even harder and with more enthusiasm than before to make up for lost time. I also returned to all of my fun activities with my large group of friends, and at that point we started calling ourselves "The Gang". In the mean time, Mr. Ross and his wife returned to New York since his contract with IBM had finished.

Ever since Mr. Thomas J. Watson, the Founder and President of IBM, who had received medals of honor from almost all the countries of the world, returned the German one to Hitler when the Germans invaded Poland and invaded and occupied most of Europe, all the offices and factories of IBM were expropriated by Hitler.

Immediately, Mr. Watson ordered that all of IBM's organization that was in the occupied Europe, figure in our accounting books in the amount of one U.S. Dollar! For that same reason, many of our functionaries in those countries were being pursued and they had to abandon their jobs and generally came to Spain to in turn continue on to the U.S. Many important people arrived in Madrid, who we had to tend to and provide them with tickets for their new destinations. Among them I remember Mr. & Mrs. Furth. Mr. Furth was until then, Director of our operations in Vienna. Others that I remember were Mr. Bader and Mr. Deroover....

With the cold weather in December came the Christmas Holidays. I decided to go to Galicia, Spain to visit my aunt Adelaida, who I had never met, since she had returned to Spain from America 37 years ago. She was an older woman - 75 years old, my mother's sister, who had married Mr. Pedreiros, but was now widowed. They did not have children. She lived by herself in a nice house and she lived very comfortably for a woman of her age.

As soon as we met, she got very attached and gave me a warm welcome and I stayed at her house. She showered me with affection. Galicia is one of the most beautiful regions of Spain. From Barallobre, where my aunt lived, I set out to visit the nearby towns: crossing La Ria, I went to Ferrol del Caudillo, birthplace of General Franco, which is an important town with its port and shipyard. Later I went to La Coruña, which is the most important city of Galicia, with its Hercules Tower, which dates back to the Phoenician times, now reconstructed after many centuries and converted to a lighthouse. I also visited the prison castle of San Anton and the Garden of San Carlos, where lay the remains of the Englishman, Johanes Moor. And lastly, I visited other nearby towns: Fene, Perlio, and Maniños which enabled me to get a good grasp of Galicia, the Beautiful. Christmas Eve and Christmas day were spent with my aunt and we went to mass at Santiago de Barallobre, where there was a beautiful nativity scene and all the children sang Christmas carols and gave their offerings. On Christmas afternoon there was a soccer game and a grand dance in the evening. The following day I left and my aunt was in tears, as she wanted me to stay longer with her. In the afternoon I took the train to Madrid, and I brought with me a large Galician bread for my friend Llopis and a Serrano ham from Mr. Asua. It was a bad trip since not only was it the coldest day of the year, 5° F, but the water pipes had broken and there was no heat in any part of the train.

The following day, on December 27 I went to the office. The 28th was the day of Holy Innocents, which is celebrated in a way similar to April Fool's Day in the United States. I was invited to a party at the home of the Marquis of Ugena and Rosa Maria directed an "Innocents" (April Fool's) play, which to me was quite new and original. Afterwards, we danced until the wee hours of the morning. On December 31st, the last day of 1940 -- a most important year for me, I went to the Alcazar Theater in the afternoon to see a play of Conchita Piquer and in the evening went with all the "Gang" to welcome the new year at the Ritz Hotel. During the dance, at midnight we ate the famous and accustomed twelve grapes for good luck, and we raised our champagne glasses and toasted. At four in the morning, this time on my own, I raised my champagne glass again and this time with my eyes shut, made a spiritual toast to all the friends I had left in Argentina, and who probably were also toasting to my health at midnight in my homeland....

My favorite church in Madrid was La Concepcion, the closest to home and my confessor was Father Jesus. Almost all of my friends from the Salamanca neighborhood would go there too. I went to mass at 12 noon to thank the Lord for allowing me to greet the new year. With some friends we later went to "Neguri" to drink some Vermouth, and then had dinner at "Chicote" and then went to dance at "Suevia". I put quotation marks on the names of places which at the time were in vogue and that possibly nowadays do not even exist. Other places that I remember that we would go to were: "Villalar", "Molinero" and "Casablanca".

Something very picturesque was taking place those days on the Gran Via - It was January 5, the day before the Three Kings Day. All the toy salesmen were lined up along that long avenue selling their wares for young and old since the following day was when everyone would indulge in their gift-giving - January 6, the Feast of the Three Kings. In other cultures, this takes place on Christmas day with Santa Claus. A few days later we had our first snow fall in Madrid, which melted a week later.

In the mean time in IBM, my work, my classes and my book were marching smoothly. At this time of year the ski season had started and with my friends, on Sundays or on holidays we would get up early and at 7:00 a.m., we would all leave on the train from the North Station to Cercedilla. From there, the sky-rail would take us to the snow peaks in Navacerrada. We would stay at the Alpine Club where we would rent the ski equipment and we would ski down the slopes of Guadarrama Mountain. In the Peñalara Club there was mass for those of us that were skiing.

On March 6, the day that I turned 31, the first thing I did that day was go to mass in the Church of San Miguel-San Benito and thank God for granting me this birthday and another year of life. I was wished a happy birthday by many friends and we celebrated together. With the Oñate and Rafecas families we went to the Queen Victoria Theater where we saw the play of the Quintero Brothers entitled "Tuyo y Mio". With these same friends a few days later we went to "La Casa de Campo". It's a large homestead that starts at the Royal Palace and that centuries ago was used as hunting grounds for the kings.

For me it was a great truth that "example is contagious". All of my friends were devote and practicing Catholics and since I was always with them, in those days we went on a spiritual retreat in the Church of Los Luises. The retreat lasted a week. Since it would start every night at 8:00 p.m., it wouldn't take time away from our daily duties and responsibilities.

"Parece que fue Ayer", title of a famous Spanish song meaning: "It seemed like yesterday" that on March 30, 1941, I had left the port of Buenos Aires a year ago with destination Spain! On April 3 it was a great day of celebration in all of Spain - Victory Day! There was a grand military parade headed by General Franco and his Guardia Mora in the Paseo de la Castellana. The Oñate and Rafecas families were very grateful to me since I invited them to see the parade from the balcony of my office, which was prime viewing.

Something very extraordinary and fantastic happened to me while I led my easy and carefree life in Madrid during those days! My friend, the attorney Antonio Laso Cana, who was married with a sister of Delia Martinez Carrero, asked me to attend a very secretive and mysterious meeting at the Café Molinero to tell me something that gave me the goose bumps. He was a lawyer for a German Insurance company in Madrid. He started by saying that since I was going out with his young sister-in-law Delia, that I had to break up

33

with her since it not only was dangerous for her, but for all her family. He confidentially told me that Madrid was a center of espionage for all the European countries that were at war, and that Germany which had helped Franco win the Civil War, had special preferential treatment from the Spanish Government. The Gestapo had extended its activities to Madrid through the "Kulturinstitut" (German Culture Institute) and through German companies like the one he worked in. He knew that many employees that were on the payroll in Madrid were members of the Gestapo and that the mission of one of them was to follow me! They thought that I was a foreigner that was living the good life in Madrid and that my real job was not with IBM, but with the Intelligence Service of England, that was at war with Germany.

It was easy to suspect this, since IBM was an American company and the U.S. was an ally with England. Frequently, the English used foreigners for their espionage and I was in and out of my office so much! It wasn't easy to convince my friend Antonio that I really did work with IBM and I had no hidden agenda. I did such a good job at convincing him that he gave me all sorts of tips on the man that was following me, and who had been doing it for quite a long time. I continued going out with Delia, and I would be careful to not make any wrong moves.... It was easy to discover my man, sometimes seated at a nearby table at a café, or in the seat behind me at the movies or at the theater. Or, when I would arrive home at the wee hours of the morning, I would catch a glimpse of him at the corner watching to see who I would arrive home with. Because of the war, my mail would always be censured, but I noticed that lately the censure was more intense than normal.

As I mentioned before, I had left my girlfriend in

Argentina, with whom I had continual correspondence. Our mail was always opened and censured by at least three different entities - the English in Gibraltar, the German Kultur-institut and the Spanish Security Direction. They were very good at it and would read the mail, erase with ink whatever they thought to be dangerous, they would seal it back and mark their name as the censuring agent. When I found out that I was being followed, and since I had a clean conscience, I decided I would make the best of it and make fun of them while I was at it. In my letters to her I would start out with phrases such as: "You shouldn't be surprised that this letter is so serious and discrete, but the thing is that I have this guy, the one who follows me everywhere, looking over my shoulder right now reading what I write." This craftiness, together with the looks that I would give the guy when I would find him sitting close to me, in any café around the city, as if saying "Why don't you come and sit with me and talk?", made them realize that I was an innocent bystander and that I had nothing to hide. Little by little, they left me alone and this truculent episode that I went through in my life had ended for good...

During these days I received an urgent communication from our IBM Headquarters in New York: That when I finished my mission in Spain, IBM needed me in Venezuela. I would first have to go to New York for training to update me on the newest inventions, and then I would continue to Venezuela without going to Argentina. I couldn't say no to this offer and discard what appeared to be a brilliant career with this company. The major obstacle that I had was the girlfriend that I had left in Argentina to which I had promised returning in a year. Over a year had already gone by, and time and distance had cooled things off already. It wasn't fair that she continue to wait for me and I took the painful decision to relieve her of this commitment...

Goya 75 was my favorite address. There was where the great Oñate family lived, and I was a friend of all of the members of this family. Together we went to all the cities near Madrid: Toledo, Segovia, Avila, Aranjuez, but my favorite place was the Escorial, because not only was it a grand monument to the Spanish Monarchy, but it was where this family had their large chocolate factory and we would always finish our evenings dancing at Matias Lopez's place. I was very interested in horse racing and I had the pleasure of going to the grand opening of the El Pardo racetrack. It was splendid, and I would also go to the Zarzuela racetrack, where once I was seated very close to General Franco, but where many a times I left my pesetas behind. Also, with my beloved friends, on June 14 we partied until sunrise on the feast of Saint Anthony with celebration and dancing. I remember hearing the morning before all the people on the streets in their pilgrimage toward the monastery of San Antonio de la Florida, most of them young seamstresses dressed and adorned in their scarves and mantillas, on their way to ask the saint to grant them a boyfriend...

By all that I have mentioned above, it would seem that my trip to Spain was not to work, but to have fun. What happened was that ever since I was a lad, I was taught to love our "mother country" through history and literature. And after reading Don Quijote de la Mancha, I entered Spain with a sort of spiritual connection and with the desire to see the windmills, or the Posada de La Sangre. I could see IBM in many parts of the world; But Spain and its people it was only now and here. That is why I wanted to document it and forge it in my memory, in the event that I wasn't going to see it again! But IBM was always first and foremost in my life. I would work day and night to accomplish my goals. It was now the month of July, which is the time when Madrid is empty since most of its people leave on vacations to escape the unbearable heat of the capital to go to their farms, or to the beautiful beaches on the coasts, only returning at the end of August.

Knowing this and also knowing that my moment of departure from Spain was getting nearer, I decided to accelerate my work. I not only wanted my students to learn theory but I wanted them to acquire experience, so I therefore assigned each one of them to assist a veteran technician to spend every morning with them. I also added an extra hour of class in the afternoons. This way we finished the course and also managed to increment by two-fold the service to our customers. Me and my managers were very happy with the results. I also finished the technical book I was writing and I gave a copy of it to each one of my students.

IBM had bought months ago my return ticket to New York, via Cuba. It was a Spanish ship, the "Magallanes", that would leave the port of Vigo in Galicia on August 7, 1941. This arrangement was good as it would give me the opportunity to visit my aunt Adelaida who lived close to Vigo, and say good-bye to her before embarking to America. The extraordinary thing was that almost every day I would receive a phone call from someone offering to buy my ticket at any price. They would offer two, and even three times the purchase price of the ticket. Usually it was people trying to escape from Hitler and the war, or people with leftist ideas who wanted to leave Franco's Spain...

In Madrid I had the pleasure of meeting an interesting person who was a friend of our "Gang". His name was

Admhed Benani, who was finishing his college studies there. He was a romantic poet, both in Arabic and Spanish. He dressed very elegantly and was the son of an important and rich Muslim family that lived in Tetuan, in the north of Africa. Admhed had invited me several times to go visit him in Morocco, before I returned to America. Since I had finished my job in Madrid, I decided to take my vacations there and in the south of Spain, which I hadn't seen yet. I took the night train from the Atocha Station toward Algeciras, where I arrived the following day in the afternoon. I then took a ship to the port of Ceuta and we arrived at sundown. I stayed at the Hotel Atlante and I remembered that my friend, General Coll lived in Ceuta. He had two beautiful daughters. I visited with him that evening and we had a grand evening.

The following day I arrived at Tetuan and I stayed at the National Hotel. Asmhed came to pick me up and took me to the Jalifa horse stables, to the Moorish and Jewish neighborhoods and we ended up at the casino. The following day we drove with a general friend of his to Tanger, which is a very important and cosmopolitan city, and since it was Friday, we finished the day in a Muslim party. I also visited the city of Xauen, which has a completely Moorish population and which is famous for its carpet factories.

Asmhed, whom I met wearing the latest styles of European attire, in his land only wore Moroccan attire, his Moorish robe and fez. He took me to a mosque, where we left our shoes at the entrance, and I watched him as he prayed facing Mecca. He would philosophize and talk with me with full honesty, telling me that in his opinion, centuries ago his civilization was very ignorant and fanatic in religious matters. They don't eat pork or get drunk because Mohammed told them that it was a sin. The truth was that in those times pork produced plagues of trichinosis and intoxicating beverages weakened the mind, and the body movements used while praying at the mosque were physical exercises to keep them in good shape. Asmhed added "All this contributed to having strong and healthy armies when we fought and conquered Spain. But I know that it is not a sin, and that is why when I was with you in Madrid, I would have my drinks and eat pork"...

In those days Asmhed was somewhat annoyed with his father, because although he had six wives, he had remarried for the seventh time with a woman much younger than he. Nevertheless he invited me to stay at the Arab palace where they lived, to have tea in the Moorish way, sitting on the floor on big fluffy pillows, served by young girls that would bring us exotic delicacies. For me this was a different world that brought to my mind the stories of the thousand and one nights...

The time arrived to leave towards my western world and to say goodbye to my friend Asmhed. A plane took me to the city of Seville. This was the first time that I traveled in a commercial plane even though I had flown in an aircraft when I was still a boy in the decade of the twenties. I remember that when we got out of school, with two or three friends we would go to a small private airport at the "Dike". There in a shed, a young pilot by the name of Estegui, kept his aircraft. We would help him push his apparatus towards the landing strip; and as done with automobiles before the electric starter was invented, you had to use a handle and also turn the propeller in order for the motor to start. As a prize for the help we gave him, our friend Estegui would take us for a ride in his aircraft over the city. Estegui was our idol, and some time later he enrolled in the Spanish Aviation, when that country had an armed conflict in Morocco. We were desolate when we read in the papers that Estegui had died in combat...

I arrived at the airport in Seville and stayed in the Hotel Cristina of that city. Since I did not have friends there, accompanied by a guide I saw almost everything that there is to see in this interesting Andalusian city: the Cathedral, the Alcazar, the Parque de Maria Luisa, the Barrio Santa Cruz, the Barrio Triana, the Virgen de la Macarena, etc. But what most caught my attention was when I visited the Archivo de Indias, I read an original letter written by none other than Miguel Cervantes y Saavedra, asking the King for a humble public job. At night I would go to the famous "tablados" of gypsy dancing.

Since I had friends in Malaga, I took a train that got me there in a few hours. I stayed at the Vasconia Hotel, and my friend Jorge Felices took charge of introducing me to his friends. Together we went to the beach Playa Del Carmen, where there was a night carnival with a dancing contest. I won the tango competition with my partner from Malaga, Paquita! Since Jorge had a canoe, we would go to the "Bateria del Faro" to row and swim at those beaches, and at night we would continue dancing! But the time came to say goodbye to "Malaga la Bella" and Paquita...

The night express took me back to Madrid, where I arrived the next morning. Since I had already given up my apartment, I stayed for a few days at the Hotel Peñon, near my office. I started to say goodbye to our customers and my friends, who just about every day gave me a small party. Thursday the 31st of July arrived, day in which I had to leave. At midday IBM offered me a banquet at the Hotel

Nacional, attended by the executives and my ex-alumni. Mr. De Asua, gave a speech praising my work and he gave me as a gift a chronometer in which the name of the company was engraved. I thanked him with few words since I was seized with emotion. Mr. De Asua and some of those present accompanied me to the Estacion del Norte to catch my train. The big surprise was for everyone as we arrived at the platform in front of my sleeper coach.

All of my gang of friends was there waiting for me with songs! Then each one came up to me, recited a farewell verse, gave me a gift followed by a hug. And like this, one after the other, after the other,... and at the end Mr. Fernando De Asua, the aristocrat, who saw the class of people seeing me off, came close to me and quietly said, " What a double secret life of yours, the best of Spain is giving you this farewell!" When I got on the train, a man that was observing from a window asked me, "Are you an actor?" I answered "No, why?" To which he answered "Because here, these types of farewells are given to actors, after a long and great act"...

My train arrived at Barallobre the next day, about noon. There my Aunt Adelaida was waiting for me and took me to her house. During the two days that I spent with my aunt she begged, almost crying, for me to stay with her, telling me that everything she owned would be for me. What for my dear aunt appeared to be an easy decision, was impossible for me; I had to part and continue the course that I had planned. We both cried when we said goodbye. One year later my aunt left this world...

Before embarking at the port of Vigo, I wanted to see some of the beautiful cities of Galicia. First I went to Santiago, where I spent the day with my friend J. A. Cimadevilla. From there to Villagarcia, and later by train to Pontevedra, where I spent almost all day at the beach, where I feasted on a grand crab. On another train I arrived to the city of Vigo and stayed at the Hotel Continental. The next day on an electric train I went to the town of Bayona, to visit my friend Pita Brandon. Together we went to the castle and that night I returned to Vigo. On the following morning the ship "Magallanes" entered the port of Vigo, coming from Bilbao. Although I was to embark the following morning I went aboard to see the ship. In the afternoon, I went to confession at the Colegiata, and the next day, August the seventh, after mass and communion in the church of Santiago, I set out towards America...

The ship was very comfortable but crowded, primarily with Jews and political refugees. I was assigned a table in the dining room with two Mexicans and a Spaniard, and we had a great time during our voyage. Also traveling with us was Monsieur Cointreau, representative of the dynasty that bears his name, and that for the last century, manufactures the famous and exquisite French liquor. Since his factory was occupied by the Germans, he brought with him the secret manufacturing formula, and started production in the United States far better than that in France. I sent radiograms thanking IBM of Spain and my gang, starting with Rosa Maria.

Navigation was good and with a calm sea. On the second night we sighted the lighthouse of the Azores. The pool was magnificent and we passed a good part of the day swimming. On Sunday morning there was a well attended nine o'clock mass. Every night there was a dance, frequented by young people. As we traveled south the heat would increase. On the 15th of August, day of the Virgin Mary, we had a grand mass sung by the tenor singer Roberto Silva.

42

That night we had a big party organized by the Red Cross, there were theatrical acts with amateurs and professionals in charge. Another night was the farewell gala, organized by Captain Celestino Aguirre Olozaga, which ended at dawn with the best dance of the voyage. One of the passengers composed the following verse for the occasion:

> At the captains party... a tear drops...
> From Bilbao we all parted on the Magallanes,
> Good passage, horses and some small canines,
> a very good captain,
> whom we will miss,
> whose party we are celebrating with summer heat bliss.
>
> Much whiskey we have drunk on this long folly,
> from eating we have not felt melancholy,
> but let us not speak of sadness,
> everything has been vociferous,
> great cries, good liquors and much laughter,
> a goat on the menu the day after;
> with cocoa the first class chocolate we get,
> but never a dispute on deck,
> in the pool we have played,
> and with the heat almost everyone has bathed.
>
> Goodbye "Capi" dearest,
> when will we see you again,
> quickly bound towards Havana
> before we get some rain.
>
> Goodbye with my heart,

for with my mouth I cannot,
my palate can only pant,
from all that I have drank. Goodbye.. goodbye...

Suddenly, one morning we began seeing on our left a small Bahaman island, and in the afternoon the Grand Bahama. It is the first land that we saw since the Azores. With the heat increasing we started to navigate through the strait of Florida, and that very same night we arrived at the port of Havana. Seeing that we would be anchored for three days here before going on to New York, some of us went on land and toured through this beautiful city.

In the morning I went to visit the IBM office of Cuba and there I met with its manager, Mr. Marcial Digat. Marcial is a person that deserves special mention. Before joining IBM he was secretary to President Machado. During many years he handled the interests of the company, until Fidel Castro took over and confiscated all of the North American companies. Marcial then, with only a few dollars in his pocket, abandoned all his valuable possessions in Cuba and joined the IBM family of New York. From there, he was determined to pull out of Cuba the best employees. He did, and placed them in various Latin American countries where they ended up having better jobs than what they had within IBM of Cuba.

Getting back to my first encounter with Marcial, he treated me like an old friend. Together with his wife Anita and young daughter Mimi, we went to his beach house and we bathed in the ocean. Marcial and his assistant Nuñez showed me the best of Havana. On the last night, I invited a lady who I met on board to see Havana at night. We had dinner at the Paris Restaurant, later we went to the Tropicana, which was the best cabaret-casino in the Caribbean. Since we were bored of so many days spent aboard ship, that night we stayed at the Hotel Nacional...

The next day when the ship set off towards New York, Digat and Nuñez were there to bid me farewell. Half of the passengers stayed in Cuba. We returned again through the Florida straits - it was hot and stormy. One could see many ships navigating through the straits. On Sunday, August the 24th, after mass we arrived in New York. First we went to Ellis Island to inspect luggage and documentation, where we stayed for two hours. Some of the passengers were detained on that island.

CHAPTER THREE

IN NEW YORK

After stepping on dry land in Manhattan I checked into the Waldorf Astoria. That same evening, with two traveling companions, my friend Bringas and his wife, we went up the Empire State Building to see the city by night and afterwards attended the show at Radio City. The next morning Mr. Peabody from IBM called me. I went to the office at 590 Madison Avenue, where I was met by Mr. Burton who introduced me to the big boss, Mr. Joseph Wilson, who handled the foreign division, the 69 countries outside of the United States. Mr. Wilson was a good-natured man who inspired trust from the very first moment. Many years before IBM was founded, he had collaborated with Mr. Hollerith, the inventor of our machines. After an animated talk about Europe and the war, Mr. Wilson ordered Mr. Burton, "You must take Luis out tonight to have a good time, so he may forget the difficulties he went through in Europe..."

Without hesitation, Mr. Burton made good use of the very generous expense account that IBM disposes of in these situations. After dinner at a good restaurant, he took me to a couple of cabarets, where he was a known customer, and always at our table were two pretty young ladies accompanying us, drinking and dancing...

The next day at the office I met up with Mr. Ross, whom I had met in Spain, and together with Mr. Blumquist we went out for lunch. In the afternoon Mr. Peabody accompanied me to the Lacawana Train Station where I would depart towards the IBM factories to initiate my studies. At the city of Binghamton Mr. Keedy was waiting for me, and took me in his car to Endicott and checked me into the Frederick Hotel. Endicott was the most important place that IBM had not only for education, but also for the production of its machines.

Mr. Van Borden was the Educational Director at the big building of Endicott. He welcomed me in his office and then took me to the most important and highly attended class that was being given at that moment. He politely interrupted and introduced me to all of the students, who were singing songs dedicated to IBM before beginning their classes. Although I didn't belong in this school, I was to stay at the same hotel for a period of time. I met a Mexican by the name of Paez Paliza who was doing a study there similar to mine. Together we went to the factory to see the latest invention, the 405 Net Balance Tabulator. That same night we put on our black-tie and attended the Gala Dinner at the IBM Country Club, where the technicians of the I.T.R. Division were graduating.

IBM had its own country club there, where employees and customers played golf for free and practiced all kinds of sports. In Endicott there was also the "Homestead", a mansion of old lineage, where some of our customers lived while taking courses and where guests would lodge. There was also a "suite" there for Mr. Watson. Something like a presidential suite at a luxurious hotel.

At the sales school, which was the most important in those days, there were some people from Latin America studying there, which I became very friendly with. Alberto Laverde from Colombia, Rogelio Alfaro from Panama, Abad from Cuba, Barriga from Bolivia, and Braun from Mexico. We celebrated together the long Labor Day weekend that started on Saturday August 30th and ended on Monday evening. Mr. Limper invited a few of us to go on an excursion. We went in two automobiles to Watkins Glen, where we had lunch; afterwards we saw an American football game at Cornell University in Ithaca, on our way back we dined at the Homestead. On Monday Mr. Klein, manager of our hotel, took us to a piece of land that he had on the shores of a lake in the state of Pennsylvania. We aquaplaned, which is similar to aquatic skiing but on a board. We had a great time doing all kinds of activities and we had dinner there. Almost every weekend the company organized outings. I remember once we all went in four big buses to Lake Seneca.

With Paez Paliza we went back to the factory, but on this occasion to study the Bank Proof, a new machine designed especially to service banks. We then continued with the new Collator. In Endicott the only large industry was IBM, in which alcoholic beverages were prohibited. In Johnson City, the neighboring town, there was a big shoe factory called Johnson's Shoes. We would go there to have fun and dance at the Pavilion. Since drinking was permitted there and they knew that our slogan was "Think", they invented a short phrase making fun of us that went "While you think we drink."

From the beginning, Alberto Laverde, who was studying at the sales school, was my best friend. Although we were about the same age, he was much more serious than I. He had married recently, and his wife who lived in Bogotá, was going to have their first child. We often went to mass and the movies together. At some point he said "Too bad that you are going to Venezuela and not Colombia, for in

49

my country we need a person like you." Moreover, I met a Mexican woman, her name was Blanca, and whenever we could, we would go and have a good time and dance at the Pavilion in Johnson City...

I continued going everyday to the factory to study all the new devices, among them, the Mark Sensing. This new invention consisted of our machine reading the marks of a pencil, as well as the holes on the card. When my time was almost up studying at this factory, Mr. Wilson called me from New York and told me that in the evening he would arrive at the Homestead for dinner accompanied by a Minister of Finance from a Latin American country. He invited me to eat with them, since Mr. Wilson didn't speak Spanish and the Minister spoke no English. With pleasure I accepted, and during the meal, Mr. Wilson asked me if I didn't have any inconvenience in changing my travel plans, that if instead of going to Venezuela I could go to Colombia to replace an American that was returning. I answered that I was in accordance. They stayed that night at the Homestead and I returned to my hotel. When I told Alberto what happened, he got very happy because we would work together in the city of Medellin.

My itinerary included another short visit to the typewriter factory in the city of Rochester. I said goodbye to my friends and took a train from the city of Binghamton. I was greeted at the station in Rochester and put up at the Hotel Seneca. That evening I was invited to dinner by the manager of the factory, Mr. Sheridan. The next day, Sunday morning, Mr. Sheridan and his wife picked me up in their car and took me to Niagara Falls. There we took a boat that traveled over part of the river. Because the wind brought rain from the falls, we were given special raincoats on the boat to protect ourselves. After lunch we crossed the Canadian border and we went for a ride through the highways of that beautiful country.

I was in Rochester for three days, the heart of our EWM Division, where the best electric typewriters were made. I left on a night train for New York and I arrived at eight thirty in the morning. I checked into the New Weston Hotel, and then went to the office where I was aided in obtaining my resident visa for Colombia. That evening Mr. Moore invited me to dinner. On the 26th of September, my last day in New York, I got up early to do my last shopping and at five in the afternoon I embarked on the "Santa Lucía" ship bound for Buenaventura, a Colombian port on the Pacific Ocean. Mr. Burton from IBM saw me off at the ship.

I noticed many North Americans on board. On the second night was the gala dance offered by the Captain. As always, during the day the main entertainment was the pool, and you could also try your aim at skeet shooting. On Sunday there was a mass on board, mostly attended by Spanish speaking people. Among them I met a Colombian by the name of Vicente Arboleda who by coincidence was also going to Medellin. And so between one dance and another, we arrived to Cristobal on the northern coast of Panama.

On that morning we took a walk through the Canal Zone in Cristobal, and we set off again to begin crossing the Canal. This was the most important part of the journey; its construction was one of the biggest feats of this century. The French who had already built the Suez Canal, started its construction and failed. Later, when the North Americans started again, the first thing that they did for the first two years was kill the mosquitoes that produced malaria, which

51

killed one in every ten workers. Fortunately, our navigation was during the day so that we were able to observe this great work of engineering. First we traveled on the Lago Gatun and then the ship started to climb Mount Culebra, through excavations and floodgates. Afterwards we descended again, towards Miraflores and Balboa, until we finally reached the city of Panama at eleven at night. Since this city had great nightlife, with a few friends we went down to experience it. My partner was Cristina and we ended up at the Cabaret Kelly.

CHAPTER FOUR

IN COLOMBIA

At nine in the morning we set off for Colombia, navigating through the Pacific Ocean. At six in the morning the following day we entered the Port of Buenaventura, in Colombia. My first impression wasn't very good. Almost all of the inhabitants of this town were black, and the only two things that existed there were the Hotel Estacion and the railroad station. I had lunch at the hotel, and at two in the afternoon I took the train towards the city of Cali. This is a railway that went along a narrow rough road up the mountain to an altitude of 4,000 feet. We arrived in Cali at eight that night. Together with two other diplomatic North American friends, en route to the Embassy in Bogotá, we checked into the Hotel Alferez Real. It was Friday, October the 3rd, and I never imagined that I was to have such a stormy weekend.

Vicente Arboleda came looking for us, and made an invitation saying "I want you to see the good and the bad of my country" and immediately called a friend and told her to prepare some good food and fine liquors; and also to bring some pretty young ladies because he would be arriving with three friends. That was an unforgettable party that lasted 24 hours without leaving that house!!

On Sunday morning I went to mass and I felt much better. On the ship I had received a radiogram from IBM of Colombia, in which I was told that at the Cali airport I would find a plane ticket going on Avianca to Medellin that morning. I arrived at eleven o'clock, and that city sounded familiar because some years before, right there, the famous Argentine singer Carlos Gardel died. Gardel's plane crashed against another plane on the same landing strip on which I had just landed. Aurelio Cerdan was awaiting me, the person I was to replace. He took me to the Hotel Europa, and together with his wife I was invited to have lunch at the Club Campestre. There I met a Mexican friend of his, Rafael Molinar, who later became a great friend of mine in Medellin.

The next day I went to our office that was very close by, on the sixth floor of a building at the Parque Berrio, in the heart of the city. Cerdan took me to meet our customers. The main one was the Railway of Antioquia, which was still being installed. The Superintendent was Mr. Neftali Sierra, an old gentleman that had specialized in the North American Railways. Within the same week Cerdan left, Mr. John Osterlund, the General Manager of IBM in Colombia, arrived with his wife from Bogotá. John was a very nice man, who aside from English, spoke perfect Spanish and Portuguese. He technically knew our business well, and was always willing to help. He stayed in Medellin just a few days and then went back to Bogotá.

I also went to Bogotá to see our main office and to get my documents in order at the immigration office. I stayed at the Hotel Granada, and had the opportunity to visit the family of my friend Laverde, who was still in Endicott and who told them that I should go visit them. I was able to meet his mother and his wife Magolita. They were a very distinguished family and were very happy to get news from Alberto. Bogotá was a city of half a million people, its inhabitants always wore overcoats and hats, because although it is in the tropics, with an altitude of 1,800 meters (6,000 feet) above sea level, the climate is cold.

From the Techo Airport, I parted again towards Medellin on a 12-passenger airplane. In this country the most common means of transportation was the airplane. The terrain is very mountainous and so there were not many roads or railways; they say that Colombia jumped from the mule to the airplane, because it was the second country in the world to have a commercial airline. After the First World War, some German pilots established a company that was called Escadta. But when the Second World War started, the United States said that it was not very convenient for these German pilots to be flying so close to the Panama Canal. So the U.S. helped Colombia found a national company, which was named Avianca, and the Germans disappeared.

I returned to the Hotel Europa and there was a courtesy card from the Club Union. This was the most important social club of the city and it was my friend Vicente Arboleda who had it sent to me. The initial bad impression that I had of Colombia upon arriving at its Pacific port totally vanished in Medellin. It had the ideal year-round temperature of 23°C (72°F). The population was only 300,000. It was the first time that I lived in a small city and I liked it. Its people were hard working and serious. Every day I tasted a new fruit that I had never known existed, and above all, its women were pretty and sweet like its fruit...

One fine day I met up with Rafael Molinar, who drove a famous car in Medellin that they called "La Cucaracha" (meaning the cockroach). It was a small Bantam convertible with two seats. Rafael shared a house with two friends who were also bachelors. When he found out that I wanted to leave the hotel, he invited me to live with them and share the expenses of the house. I accepted with pleasure, and from that moment on I formed part of a brotherhood: the Mexican Rafael Molinar, executive in a dye company; the Englishman John Castles, executive at the Socony Vacuum Oil Co.; the Swede Bengt Lindahl, executive at a paper company and the consul of Sweden; and I the Argentine with IBM. The house was big, each one had a spacious bedroom and we had three maids: the cook, the one that cleaned the house, and the one that washed the clothes. In their tidy uniforms, they would also help us out whenever we would have a party. The house and its members were serious and respectable people and known by the name of "Bottoms Up". We kept a guest book, which had the most distinguished names of the city.

I became a member of the Club Campestre, which had all kinds of sports. With my roommates we played golf, tennis, bowling or we would swim at the pool. Every Saturday night there was a dance with an orchestra, where the best of society would go. I was also invited to the Rotary Club and became a member as well; we would meet for lunch once a week at the Club Union; among its members were the most important businessmen of the city.

Meanwhile I was very busy with my work, especially with the Railways of Antioquia. I was improving the payroll method for their workers, who were then being paid weekly in cash. I invented a system by which we would automatically print envelopes with the tabulator, which were given to the workers with the money that they had made during the week. Each envelope had printed on it the name and number of the worker, the amount of hours worked, and the total value inside. If for some reason there was a delay in getting the payroll ready, I would stay working until the early hours of the morning with the head accountant, Mr. Adolfo Valencia, until the job was complete. It was imperative that it be ready at the time of the departure of the first train.

I also dedicated a lot of my time with our other customers like the State Statistical Department, or the "Almacen Universal" - with one of the owners, Mr. Tomas Santamaria. Also I worked with Mr. Vicente Restrepo from the store "La Primavera". In the meantime, Alberto Laverde Esguerra arrived in Medellin, after finishing his studies in the United States. He came with his wife and newborn son. Alberto was not only a close business associate, but also a true friend. As a Colombian who knew his country and people well, he always gave me good advice that helped me throughout my career in Colombia.

It was a big relief for me that Alberto had arrived. He immediately took charge of the office and I did what I knew best - the technical aspects of the business. Since during office hours we moved around in the same areas, Alberto and I decided to buy a car to share it half-and-half - it cost us $600 Colombian pesos. In the evenings, I would use it Monday through Friday, and he would use it during the weekends, while I was at the Club Campestre with my friends. I must confess that at first I wasn't very careful checking the car before I handed it over to them for the weekend. Alberto and Magolita would joke about the fact that sometimes they would find a piece of women's clothing in it....

In the office we had a young office boy named Quiroga. He was the youngest employee that IBM had in Colombia. He would open the office in the mornings, pick up the mail and answer the phones when we were out.

Alberto was the manager and all Medellin was his sales territory. With the good instruction that he received at Endicott,
he was dedicated to sell our three product lines with much
success, and I would install and do the maintenance on all of
these sales. Alberto and Magolita were friends of the house,
and sometimes would come and eat with us. One of those
evenings Alberto, boasting of his poetic vein, brought a gift
with the following poem:

> May the monkey I send today
> in an expression of admiration
> serve always as a mascot
> for honest imitation
> of the four playboys
> members of the Club Bottom
> Rafico the real man
> Binguito the Swede buffoon
> Juanito the smiling one
> and the gaucho Lamassonn...e

Mr. Watson, the founder of IBM, was not only a great
businessman but also a visionary. A recommendation that
he gave to all of the offices in the United States and all
around the world, was that we should be attentive to the
local contemporary art movement. If there was any piece
that we judged was good, then we should buy it to enlarge
the grand collection that IBM had in New York. One day
we met a young sculptor, Rodrigo Arenas Betancourt, who
had sculpted a wood statue called "La Minera". We let him
know that we were interested, and that he should bring his
statue to our office. He brought it wrapped in newspaper.
We bought it for 250 dollars and today it is worth millions

since this artist became the most famous sculptor of the country.

Many of the parties at the Club Campestre would continue at the house of one of its members. I remember many ended up in Ellenville, the country home of Lucíano Restrepo and his wife Ellen. Usually they finished in the pool at dawn, where we would have breakfast. Our house was so famous that we even created a "Bottoms Up Cup" to be played at the Club Campestre, exclusively for women members. A lot of times this would mean that the parties ended up at Bottoms Up, so we would end up hosting our friends, bringing the musicians to our house and the party would continue. Since Rafael played the guitar and sang, he always had friends that accompanied him. Among them, we had the honor of having in our house the famous composer Jaime R. Echavarria. He was very young and at night would come and practice with Rafael. Afterwards, we would go out and serenade our girlfriends...

We also never neglected our civic duties. There came a time when the city decided to construct a good hotel. The Government Office contributed by giving the lot of land in the Nutibara Square. All of the businessmen and citizens raised the money to build the hotel. The shares cost a peso each and in very little time it was inaugurated with the name Nutibara. For many years it was the best hotel in the center of the city. I still preserve some original shares, which have not given me dividends, but have given me great satisfaction.

As all things in life, there came the news that Alberto was being promoted to General Manager in Bogotá, and John Osterlund was transferred to management in Venezuela. Alberto's promotion was well deserved since he was so well prepared for that position. The only thing that worried me was that I had to fill the void that Alberto left behind, and at that moment they could not send me any help. In any case, I was not frightened but devoted to being a one-man band. I would arrive very early to my office, tend to the usual needs, writing and answering letters, answering the telephone and most important, following up on sales and prospective customers that Alberto had pending.

Although I was left alone with my young assistant Alberto Quiroga, the office did not fall behind; I even allowed him to leave early in the afternoons to enable him to graduate from high school. He now knew how to type, and I could dictate our business letters. In addition, I did not neglect my sports activities. From an early age I have had a passion for car racing. The Automobile Club organized the first competition on the roads around Medellin and I was the winner by a large margin. My copilot was Quiroga who was very proud because the newspapers made such a coverage of our feat. Second in line was Alejandro Echavarria, coming in 5 minutes and 46 seconds behind us.

During Christmas and New Years' our customers usually closed their businesses to take a short vacation. I took advantage and explored Colombia. I went on a train to Puerto Berrio, and there took a boat on the Magdalena River towards Barranquilla. These were river boats moved by large wheels at the stern just like the ones still used on the Mississippi, but in the tropics. On the shores of the river alligators slept and in the trees monkeys of many colors climbed. This was a feast for my eyes, as if I was watching a motion picture. In Barranquilla I stayed at the Hotel Prado, and there I saw my friends Sergio Leyva and his wife Nelly. Sergio had been appointed Governor of the State of Guajira, and was on his way there in his automobile. He invited me to accompany them and to spend some days with them at their house in Uribia. I gladly accepted, and the first part of the trip took a full day. We crossed the Magdalena River on a raft. We arrived in Valledupar, and there we stayed at Pedro Castro's home, the most important man in the region and great leader of the Liberal party. The following day, we traveled all day in infernal heat. I spent some unforgettable days among the Guajiro Indians, whose only piece of clothing was a guayuco, a cloth that hung from their waist, whose only purpose was to cover their genitals. In contrast, women wore long colorful dresses.

We went to Cabo de la Vela and we bathed in Venezuelan beaches. In Uribia there were two industries: salt extracted from the sea exploited by the Banco de la Republica, and pearl fishing done by the native Indians. They would submerge approximately eight meters, without breathing to the bottom of the sea taking a basket tied with a string. When the basket was filled with oyster shells they would give a signal with the string, and from above someone would pull the basket up. On the spot they would open the shells and almost always in each basket a very valuable natural pearl was found. We who watched could buy the pearl and take the fresh oysters home to eat.

The moment arrived to leave and Sergio offered me two methods. One on a government plane that arrived the following day, and the other that same afternoon on a boat loaded with salt that would take me to Santa Marta. I thought the latter more attractive, and so I departed riding on the shoulders of an Indian, who carried me to the boat that was waiting for me near the beach. Other than the salt, I found myself aboard with four sailors and a cook. The sea was rough because it was the windy season - what they call the "brisas".

We began navigating and from the kitchen came a wonderful aroma of grilled fish. Two hours later while the cook was serving my meal I understood that what they call brisas is a real storm! So much so that the sailors would not eat because they were dizzy, and the cook threw a good part of the food into the sea. A school of sharks followed us and as they savored the food, as always, they smiled... In spite of the movement of the boat that night, I was able to sleep some, and at dawn we entered the spectacular bay of Santa Marta. Happy with my adventure I returned to Medellin in a plane with a beautiful pearl in my pocket, which I bought from an Indian for a small amount of money and that later was transformed into a tie pin...

The Argentine consul for all of Colombia was Mr. Miguel Jordan, who resided in Bogotá, who was actually honorary consul. Miguel appointed me as his representative in Medellin. Towards the end of 1943, I was to be active in this post since this city was chosen to be the site of the first School of Meteorology. It was sponsored by the United States with the purpose of improving information for aviation in Latin America. We had an invasion of young students from different countries, who were known by the nickname of "Meteorologists". They were charming and had college education, but they were very restless and made havoc among the feminine element. The Argentines were famous for their nocturnal activities, and many times I had to get them out of jail, because of an uproar they created in places of dubious morality...

In Colombia a lot of platinum was produced in the region of Choco, which during the war ended up in the hands of Hitler, via Buenos Aires. England and the United States joined forces to investigate who were the middlemen in this activity. During these days our comrade from Bottoms Up, John Castles, was transferred and left us. Sometimes I played golf with an Englishman, Leonard England, manager of the Marconi Wireless. One fine day he told me that he was bored living where he was and wanted to move. So I invited him to come live with us and occupy the vacancy left by our friend John. He accepted with pleasure and moved in. A long time passed, and when the war was over Len told me that he had to make a confession. He said that other than working with his company, he belonged, to the British Intelligence Service. His mission in Medellin was to spy my movements, because it was thought that I was the platinum middleman, and it was easily believed for I was the only Argentine in that city. When by my own invitation, he came to live with me and it became easier for him to follow my movements. He then knew that I was not who he thought I was. He also told me that our mutual friend Jim Joyce, who supposedly represented Merrill Lynch, was the other fellow following me. Something similar to what happened to me in Spain, but the other way around...

What had to happen, happened; the first member of Bottoms Up succumbed to the charms of a Colombian woman. Rafael Molinar married Luz Pelaez and moved to Mexico. A bit later Bingo was returning to Sweden and Len, the Englishman, also left Medellin. The hour also arrived for me because I was needed in Bogotá. So, seeing that our house was dissolving, we had a grand party of mutual good-byes, which was news in all the newspapers of the city. At that party the members of Bottoms Up decided that I would keep the scrapbook of memories of our house, and that it should be continued in Bogotá. So it was, and I still have it in my possession, with additions of my social activities in Bogotá.

Although my transfer to Bogotá meant a promotion, I was to leave Medellin with great sadness, since it had been a happy piece of my life that I would never want changed. I was replaced in my job by the North American Alvaro Diaz Cervino, and his aid would be Juan Teran, a good employee from the Bogotá office who knew our machines quite well. I stayed at the Hotel Granada while I got an apartment. I immediately went to work. Alberto Laverde, who knew my abilities, placed me in charge of the Sales Department with my own customer base, the Education Department, where I would give classes, and I also supervised the Engineering Department, which was managed by Jose Joaquin Torres, the oldest employee of the company.

In my opinion, it was a very difficult task for Alberto Laverde to manage all of the activities of the company, which had many employees. Concurrently, he had to maintain communication almost on a daily basis with New York. He knew that for IBM the most important thing was to maintain good customer service and improve human relations within the personnel of the company. I was to be his right hand man and the layer of management where all the common problems would go to, which I knew well and could resolve immediately, freeing up the General Manager's time.

With all these tasks, I had to proceed with great tact so as not to step on anybody's toes. In sales I met none other than Raymond Girault, a great Frenchman who before the war worked for IBM in France. When the war broke out, he was called to arms, and fighting for his country he experienced the withdrawal from Dunkerque, where he was wounded and evacuated to England. At that time, the IBM family was in London, although battered by the German bombardments. Once Raymond recovered from his wounds IBM took charge of him. While in London he met Joyce, a beautiful young Englishwoman, and he married her. A short time later IBM transferred him and his wife to the United States. He did his sales schooling in Endicott, and since Raymond spoke some Spanish he was transferred to Colombia. At the French Embassy he was honored with the Cross of the War for fighting for his country. Sometime later, Andre, his first child and his daughter Marie Louise were born in Bogotá. These were the kind of members in my IBM family, which was becoming more international. The family ties became even closer when years later, I became the godfather of his third daughter Marie Claude, born in the United States.

We placed Bernardo Reyes as Raymond's sales assistant, a distinguished young man who we were training in sales. We assigned Carlos Salgado as my sales assistant. To improve customer service, we sent Alfonso Rosas, Jorge Gonzalez and Carlos Castellanos to an Engineering School in Argentina for six months. In the mezzanine of our office we equipped a small room, where I would periodically give classes to our customers' employees. An extraordinary thing that I recall was that some of my classes were inaugurated with a small speech, pronounced by none other than Carlos Lleras Restrepo, who later became President of the Republic of Colombia. In my free time I visited my customers and tried to generate new sales, which would give me commissions and points for the 100% Club.

I didn't neglect my social life in Bogotá either. I

rented a nice apartment very close to the office so that I did not have to take my car out to go to work. The city was small and almost everything was done by foot. Although the cable car passed right in front of our door on the Carrera Septima, I used my car when visiting customers or for prospective ones. I bought my share in the Country Club, where I was admitted as a member. This club was very elitist and the candidates for membership went through much scrutiny. This club was very close by near the Lago Gaitan on Calle 85 and Carrera 15, where I played golf with my new friends. I was also member of the Jockey Club, downtown in front of the Parque Santander and the Rotary Club as well.

The Argentine colony was very small and we were all friends of Ricardo Fernandez Mira, the eternal in charge of the Embassy, and I say eternal because the Ambassador was constantly changed but he always stayed in charge of the Embassy. Ricardo was a career diplomat famous in Bogotá for being a great tango dancer, and being very well connected, he took charge of introducing us to the few Argentines that resided in Bogotá. Among them were Ismael Arensburg, who arrived to this city in 1940. He worked for Galerias Lafayette, and produced the hair creme Lechuga. Through the Daniel Musical Society he brought to Bogotá the best Theatrical Companies and great musical virtuosos like Rubinstein or the Children's Choir of Vienna. When the artist was a friend, Ismael would put them up at his house, like in the case of our countrywoman, the reciter Berta Singerman. Many times while she recited at the Teatro Colon, we would stay with her husband and agent playing poker. Our dear friend and fellow countryman Antonio Lattanzio would also participate in these activities. He was the representative of the prestigious drug firm Abbott. Both were bachelors and both got married in the same week. Ismael with Berta Latorre and Antonio with Ines Restrepo. They had many children, which later established respectable and purely Colombian homes.

Later other prestigious Argentines came to Bogotá, such as Ramon Meira Serantes, of Spanish lineage. With his wife Perla they arrived on a diplomatic mission and they stayed here for good. After leaving diplomacy, Ramon dedicated himself to business, was a professor at the University of Santo Tomas, and now writes his weekly column in the daily paper El Siglo. A fervent Catholic, he proudly holds the Great Cross of the Order of the Holy Sepulcher of Jerusalem. In addition to other medals of various countries, in Colombia, Ramon received La Cruz de Boyaca. Ramon, Ismael and I are presently the three oldest persons born in Argentina living in Bogotá.

The operations of the office in Bogotá were going well but we couldn't say the same for Medellin. Moreover, Alvaro Diaz was returning to the United States. I had to return to Medellin until things got straightened out. Although the flight in Avianca only lasted 40 minutes, I preferred to drive my car; and even though the roads were bad, I enjoyed contemplating the tropical landscape during three days. The first stage was from Bogotá to Ibague where I spent the night, the second stage to Manizales and the last to Medellin. I stayed at the Hotel Nutibara.

During those days, the famous Spanish bullfighter Manolete and his team arrived to the city with much pomp for a series of bullfights. Between them, they occupied a whole floor at the Hotel Nutibara. Also accompanying the bullfighter was a beautiful woman, a theatre artist with purple hair. I was introduced to Manolete, who I thought was an introverted person but very charming. That Saturday I invited him together with his friend to eat and dance at the Club Campestre. He declined the invitation and said that just before a bullfight he did not stay up late; but he told me to go to the party with his girl friend. Without hesitation, I took her to the Club, where we caused great commotion, especially among the mothers of the young women I used to go out with. To avoid me any problems, my good friend Jorge Gonzalez, who was the president of the club, sat with us in order to purge the bad atmosphere that was being produced at such an elite place... The next day Manolete had a triumphal fight. A short time later, he was killed by a bull in Spain.

I got bored of living downtown and went to live at the Club Campestre. There I would get up very early, would do a round of golf with Mr. Appleby, the English golf instructor, and then I concentrated on the problems at the office for as late as it took. A short time later everything got back to normal and I was able to return to Bogotá.

I dedicated myself to recuperate time lost. I had already made contacts with the executives of the Tropical Oil Company and had been authorized to make a survey to implement our accounting machines. Although they had offices in Bogotá, their principal operation was in El Centro close to Barrancabermeja. This was in the middle of the jungle, next to the Magdalena River. I was there during fifteen days studying their organization and compiling the data to complete my study. Some time later, I presented the study that was a book one hundred pages long. My thorough project was approved and we signed the contract for 1,493 points. This was my first real big business transaction and enough to get me into the 100% Club. When the machines arrived, we installed them at the Bogotá office, and there we gave courses to their personnel. Jorge Nossa was the head of the team and everything worked very well right from the start.

Gerrit Barger, IBM General Manager for Latin America, visited us in 1945 and verified that our Colombian organization was moving along very well. When he learned that I had not taken a vacation in the last four years, he urged me to do so. I decided to take a month off and travel to Argentina.

My co-workers continued being my "IBM family", and I practiced our golden rule of good human relations with all of them. I never had a quarrel with them and all my staff appreciated and respected me. As in the past, I never mixed my personal life with my professional life, while at the same time giving my staff personal and group attention. In my Bogotá home I continued my "Bottoms Up" album, which I constantly refer to when writing these memoirs. In this book I found a page with the following invitation, which was posted on the office bulletin board by our secretary:

"On occasion of his trip to Argentina, the following 15th of December, Luis A. Lamassonne invites all the members of IBM Colombia to the farewell "Drink Party" that will take place on the 6th at 6:00 pm. This gathering will also celebrate the following events:

A. The signing of the contract with the Tropical Oil Company for 1,493 points.

B. The return of Negus of Ethiopia to the throne.

C. The graduation of his uncle, "the one who plays the violin", in Atomic Science.

D. The 223 grams of weight that Mr. Alvaro Aguirre gained during 1945.

E. The lottery that Mr. Raymond Girault won in 1943 and the one he will win in 1959, much to the merriment of the lottery ticket salesman that visits him daily.

F.

G.

H.

I.

Note: F, G, H, and I were left blank for the spontaneous collaboration of our distinguished guests, who we ask to be punctual to this event and to wipe their shoes before entering.

The party was a success. Some of the attendees came with their wives, and they all signed the book and many left personal dedications. For example I can read Joyce Girault's note: "Why don't you get married Luis?" In connection with the subject of marriage, I had my tactics: I would go out with a few girlfriends at a time so as not to get hunted down...

My friends also threw a few farewell parties for me that appeared in the social pages of the newspaper. There was another talked-about party I offered for my friend Ricardo Fernandez Mira at my apartment, with the occasion of his transfer to Cuba on another diplomatic mission.

My trip was on a "Panagra" plane leaving from the Techo Airport. All of my friends were there to see me off. It was on the best and largest aircraft of that time, a DC-3. Pressurized cabins had not appeared yet, and all passengers had to wear oxygen masks while crossing the Andes between Chile and Argentina. Since the trip had to be made in several stages, I was able to spend a few days in Lima and in Santiago.

The only family I had left in Argentina was my widowed sister and her two children. I spent most of my time with old friends in Buenos Aires and La Plata. I learned that my former girlfriend had married. My IBM family offered a dinner in my honor and it was very pleasant to see my former co-workers who wanted to know all about my new life. Benito Esmerode was the General Manager and the company had progressed enormously under his management. It was a wonderful feeling to be back in my old stomping grounds after five years! I saw the old Gimnasia y Esgrima Club, the University Club and the Sarmiento Association where I donated my time, together with other generous friends, teaching Spanish to poor immigrants. The days and hours passed so quickly while I revisited my sweet childhood memories.

I returned to my work routine in Colombia. We continued to increase our customer base and opened a branch office in Barranquilla, where Raymond Girault got even more customers. Around that time Raymond went on vacation to the United States with his family. Since he bought a car there, he decided to have his family return by plane, while he came back to Barranquilla by ship with his new car. From there he sailed down the Magdalena River and enjoyed a very picturesque adventure with the steam wheel paddle ship going down river to a port near Bogotá. I had already traveled down the Magdalena River when it was a tropical paradise, where you could see alligators sleeping along the shorelines. Since Raymond was not experienced driving on Colombian roads, I drove my car to meet him in Puerto Salgar, and we drove from there up to Bogotá, making our way up the winding mountain roads.

Mauricio Obregon was an important character in Bogotá. I called him the Colombian Magellan. In spite of

71

his youth, Mauricio had already traveled the world by land, sea and air. He flew his own small plane and we enjoyed inviting girlfriends on short flights. Sometimes I provided the ladies and he provided the plane. Among them I remember the two lovely daughters of Celso Vargas, Ambassador of Chile in Colombia. Later on, Mauricio married and gained international fame with his travels and discoveries in world map making.

Continuing with our daily routine, one morning Raymond asked me to have lunch with him because his wife was having lunch at home with her friends. We went to a downtown restaurant called Monte Blanco. It was on a second floor and we had a window table facing Carrera Septima, a major avenue in Bogotá. Towards the end of our meal we heard the sound of gunshots, and as we looked down into the street, we saw a man shooting another man as he walked along the street with two friends. A police officer immediately apprehended the attacker while the two men looked after their injured friend. Immediately two shoe shine boys ran out of a café and grabbed the attacker from the police officer's control, and began to hit him on the head repeatedly with their shoe shine boxes. As the injured man's friends took him away in a taxi to the hospital, the shoe shiners dragged the attacker along the street and beat him to death. Both the man who had been shot and his attacker died a few minutes later. We had just witnessed a major political assassination. It was April 9, 1948, and Jorge Eliecer Gaitan, the People's Leader, had just been killed in front of our very eyes...

As we left the restaurant, a mob gathered and took over the streets, breaking windows and looting shops, stealing weapons and liquor. It was the beginning of a revolution that was later named "el Bogotazo" because it occurred at the same time as the Pan-American Conference in Bogotá, attended by General Marshall. The conference was being held in the congressional buildings, and IBM had installed simultaneous interpretation equipment for the event. We brought technicians in from Endicott as well as several female interpreters from the United Nations. They were all staying at the Hotel Granada, which unfortunately was located right in the center of the mob and civil commotion. The Armed Forces took control of the city, and the government decided to move the conference away from the Congressional buildings to the Gimnasio Moderno, a school building in a much safer area for all of the important conference delegates from around the Americas. A curfew was imposed, and only vehicles with official clearance were allowed to circulate in the streets. I was able to get clearance, and drove downtown to find my staff so that we could clear all of the interpretation equipment out of the area. There was no one left in the hotel when I got there, but they had left me notes telling me that they were seeking safety at friends' homes. Three days later, when the government regained control of the city, we were able to move the equipment and the conference reconvened. I was friends with the Argentine Ambassador, Pedro Juan Vignale, and he invited me to stay at the Embassy, which was now a safe place. This was thanks to General Peron, who sent a plane-load of food and supplies from Argentina, as well as an Army Officer and seven soldiers to protect the Embassy. After much coming and going, when things returned to normality I found two bullet holes in my car, shot by snipers.

After April 9, the paradise that I had first known in 1941 was never the same. Liberals and Conservatives began killing each other for reasons of political rivalry, and now we have a guerrilla war that is rampant throughout the entire country!

Shortly thereafter, my friend Raymond was relieved and happy to leave Colombia, and was transferred to New York. That same year I spent a few days in his New Jersey home during a vacation in the United States. Before leaving Colombia I made arrangements with an automobile agency in the U.S. to pick up a new convertible at the factory. I visited my IBM family in New York and they made a reservation for me and my new car on a Grace Line ship. For those of us who enjoy driving, it is such a pleasure to "floor" the accelerator on those great American highways after so much driving on bad roads. I drove all the way to Canada, and after two weeks, I returned to my New York office. There I met Mr. Wilson, who had me pose with him for a portrait with a "100 Percent Club" badge, as I had already exceeded my sales goals for the year. When I was ready to return to Colombia, I got the bad news that my ship couldn't sail because of a New York Port workers strike.

There was no way to know when the strike would end, and I had business to tend to in Colombia and had to return on a set date. I contacted my friend Elena Martinez Mendoza who was the Colombian Consul in New Orleans. Elena made a reservation for me on a ship that would leave three days later, from New Orleans to Buenaventura. The difficult task would be for me to drive 2,500 kilometers (1,550 miles) on my own. My office contacted the Automobile Association to see if they could find me a driving partner for this long journey. They were not successful and advised me to see the hotel doctor to get medication to keep me awake during the long drive. I was staying at the Commo-

74

dore, and made an appointment with the hotel doctor. He gave me a full physical check up, and a prescription for Benzedrine, warning me not to take it too frequently. I packed a trunk and two suitcases, and two hotel porters loaded them in the trunk and back seat of my new car. That same night I left New York, bound for New Orleans.

I have never driven non-stop for such a long time. I only stopped for gas, coffee and pills. On the second day I stopped and bought a "chicken in a basket" and a few bottles of Coca-Cola. While I drove at 120 kilometers per hour (75 mph) that chicken tasted like heaven. Fortunately, I was only stopped once by a police officer for speeding. I exaggerated my South American accent, told him of my predicament and showed him my international driver's license. He took pity and allowed me to continue, on the condition that I slow down...

I arrived in New Orleans just in time to find Elena, pay for my ticket, load the car on the ship and invite her to dinner. Shortly thereafter, I was off to Colombia, but due to the pills I had taken, I suffered severe depression and slept all the way to the Panama Canal. I woke up for meals that the crew brought to my cabin, and then went back to sleep. When we arrived in Panama City, I felt rejuvenated and got off the ship to have some fun. This time when we arrived in Buenaventura, everything felt more familiar. I watched my car get unloaded by crane, and after paying the customs duties for the car (only $800 pesos back then), drove to Cali on a very bad road. I managed to do it quicker than by train. I stayed in Cali for a couple of days, researching the possibility of opening an IBM branch office there. I woke up very early and drove all day in order to arrive in Bogotá by sunset. It was wonderful to arrive in my apartment and sleep in my old familiar bed...

It was very fortunate that Elena Martinez Mendoza was the Colombian Consul in New Orleans, and that thanks to her I was able to return in time to fulfill my obligations. Elena belonged to a distinguished Bogotá family, and I was a friend of her mother's, her two sisters, Rosita and Carmen, and her cousin Cecilia. All of them signed their names and wrote some thoughts in my guest book. I was also a friend of their cousin, Santiago Martinez Delgado, a great painter. When Santiago was young, he was rummaging through his cousins' attic, and among some old dusty paintings he discovered an original Raphael. This painting was sent to the United States for verification, restoration and sale.

I had learned confidentially in New York that 1949 was going to be a very special year for IBM in Latin America, and I therefore concentrated on ensuring that IBM Colombia would meet all sales goals. We opened our third branch office in the city of Cali, and this contributed to our progress. In the same year, Carlos Vidal was named special representative for Latin America, and he was a great promoter of IBM in this part of the world. Vidal was Peruvian, and he not only developed IBM business in his own country, but now traveled all over the continent, maintaining his office in Peru.

Around the same time was the much publicized arrival in Bogotá of Barbara Jean Floyd, "Miss New Orleans 1948", a beautiful 18 year old. My friend Jaime Restrepo, assistant to his father, Mr. Fabio Restrepo (General Manager of the newspaper "El Tiempo"), was in charge of the publicity for this event. Jaime and I were determined that this young beauty queen have a good time, and we arranged many events and parties in her honor. Here she met George Cauthen, an airline pilot and married him, but their marriage only lasted two weeks. Their divorce in the United States also got a great deal of publicity... I can see in my scrap book two pages from Life Magazine with all the details of their separation, as well as a lovely dedication that Jean wrote in my guest book when she visited my apartment.

Meanwhile, IBM was moving full speed ahead and by mid-year we had met our quotas for the entire country, and I had met my personal sales goals. What I had heard confidentially in New York was now a widespread rumor. In early 1950 the first major Latin American Convention would be held in Rio de Janeiro, chaired by Mr. Watson. All of those who had met their sales quotas were invited, as well as each country manager.

I heard that Raymond Girault was traveling to IBM Puerto Rico and Jamaica. Since I had never visited either one of these islands, I decided to take a short vacation and meet Raymond in Puerto Rico. Thomas Watson Junior, son of the founder of IBM and Tom Kirkland, who were both vice-presidents of the company happened to be in Puerto Rico. There was a large company dinner with all of the staff of IBM Puerto Rico, and I was invited. Watson Junior made the keynote speech, and he mentioned me as an example, saying that IBM must be very important in my life in order for me to be present at a company dinner rather than relaxing during my vacation.

After that, Raymond and I went to Jamaica. He was working and I was still on vacation and we parted ways in Kingston, where I continued on to Ocho Rios and then to Santo Domingo in the Dominican Republic. After touring all of the beautiful historical areas of the city, I spent my time at the hotel swimming pool. I met a lovely young lady who was staying at the same hotel. We dined, danced and had a wonderful time together until the day a man knocked at my door and very seriously told me that I shouldn't see her again. He warned me that if I continued pursuing her, my life would be in danger! He informed me that the young lady had been brought there for Trujillo, the dictator. Later on I learned that Trujillo had people all over the world that found women for him. I accepted the man's advice and returned to Colombia almost immediately. Not long after that Trujillo was assassinated on his way to one of his trysts.

From my vacation in the islands I brought back a few records of tropical music that were very fashionable at the time. Towards the end of the year I met my friend Alfonso Hernandez Osuna who asked me to bring my new records to a party he was having at his home on January 4, 1950. I knew Alfonso since he was single, and he now lived in a large home with his whole family. At his party I was introduced to people of all ages and varied backgrounds. One of Alfonso's sisters sat at the piano and sang soprano. But there was one special person who from the beginning made my heart beat faster. Her name was Lucía Medina Sierra, and she had just returned from completing her studies in Canada. It seemed like the feeling was mutual and we spent the entire evening together. After dinner, an informal roulette was organized and I told Lucía we could play my money together, and then split the earnings. I think we were the only winners, and at the end of the evening we split the money as easily as possible: one for you, one for me... when we got to the last five peso bill I ripped it in half and told her that we would have to get together again for that last torn bill to be worth something. I gave her my telephone number and she gave me hers. From then on we saw each other every day until it was time for me to leave for the IBM convention in Rio de Janeiro.

The convention was a major event. Carlos Vidal and IBM Brazil prepared it very well. Even though IBM wives didn't participate in the convention, almost all of the married attendees brought their wives along and arranged private tours for them. Mrs. Watson always accompanied her husband when he traveled and Alberto Laverde brought his wife Magolita with him. Since I couldn't get Lucía off my mind I decided to find time to visit Mr. Stern in his jewelry store and buy her a diamond ring. When the convention was over, Alberto, Magolita and I flew to Buenos Aires, but I quickly returned to Bogotá to make arrangements for the arrival of Mr. And Ms. Watson in Colombia. As they never traveled by plane, they continued by ship to Buenos Aires, then by land to Chile, and from there by sea on the Pacific all the way to Buenaventura.

Since we already knew that the visit to Colombia would only be for one day, their ship docked in Buenaventura; we had already inspected the only hotel where we could hold the reception: the Hotel Estacion! We found it in complete shambles, and had to arrange to renovate and paint the dining room, as well as change all of the curtains. When I arrived in Bogotá with the person in charge of all of the arrangements, we even had to buy the china that would be used at the luncheon ourselves. We hired Alfonso Castillo, a friend from the Circle of Journalists, to organize all of the publicity and travel to Buenaventura to interview Mr. Watson.

During my entire trip Lucía and I communicated on a daily basis, and when I returned to Bogotá we saw each other every day. One night while we were dining at the Hotel

Granada I placed the ring I purchased in Rio de Janeiro on her finger. When she showed it to her father he said: "my child, this is an engagement ring", and Lucía replied: "well, yes we are engaged". From that moment, I abandoned my old habits of dating several women at once and dedicated myself to her alone...

As the saying goes: if Mohammed doesn't go to the mountain, the mountain must come to Mohammed. As soon as Alberto returned from Argentina we began preparations to transport all of the IBM Colombia staff to Buenaventura, leaving only the minimum staff needed in each city to provide basic services to our customers. We all traveled to Cali by plane, and from there by train to Buenaventura. The next morning the ship arrived from Valparaiso and a reception committee formed by those of us who spoke English (and a few IBM wives) welcomed Mr. and Mrs. Watson, as well as Carlos Vidal who had arrived with them. Against our advice, Mr. Watson insisted on taking a tour around the town. A few of us accompanied them and each time we encountered a group of naked black children, Mr. Watson told us that we were "all guilty of this social injustice". After a wonderful lunch, Mr. Watson addressed the group while Carlos Vidal interpreted and took notes. As usual, it was more than a speech, it was wise advice; not only advice for business but also for human relations. In the afternoon, he and his wife invited us to tea in one of the dining rooms on board the ship. In the early evening they sailed to New York, via the Panama Canal. The staff of IBM Colombia spent the night at the Hotel Estacion, and the next morning we all made our way back home. We have wonderful photographs from this event, which represented quite a large expenditure for IBM Colombia.

We returned to our work routine and my relationship with Lucía was each day more serious and more loving. One day I invited her father, Mr. Arturo Medina to lunch, and told him of my intention to marry his daughter, who was then 19 years old. Since he didn't respond immediately, I continued in a joking manner, telling him that it would be a mutually convenient arrangement, because not only were we very much in love, but I was also committed to taking care of his daughter and his grandchildren. He agreed, smiling...

We received a visit from Carlos Vidal who informed me that the company was giving me a promotion. It was time to develop our business in Central America and I would be named Manager in El Salvador. I told Lucía and asked her if she would like us to get married in Colombia and then move to that part of the world. I knew that she would agree and that we would start our first great adventure together. We set a date for our wedding, July 26, 1950, and on that same day we would leave on our trip to Central America. We began to prepare for this important event, and obtained tickets and visas for all of the countries we would travel through, from Costa Rica to Mexico. We planned to spend our honeymoon in Mexico and then establish our residence in El Salvador.

The last few days before the wedding were very hectic with church arrangements, civil registration, and farewell parties. At the last party offered by my friends, there were many speeches and finally when my turn came I ended my speech saying "I'm getting married tomorrow but I promise I'll never do it again". On the afternoon before our wedding I went to the office to say goodbye to my co-workers and clear my desk. Our English-speaking secretary, Miss Margaret Meier informed me that a confidential telegram had arrived from New York for me. It was from the Big Boss, and it more or less said the following: "Congratulations on your wedding tomorrow. Cancel all of your travel plans and get residence visas for you and your future wife to live and work in New York." The first thing I did was call Lucía and ask her: "If we didn't go to Central America, where would you want to go?" And she replied "New York". My response to her: "Well that's where we're going!". Then I told her all about the telegram.

Since we couldn't change our wedding plans, but we could change the travel plans, I called my travel agent and told him to cancel all of our travel arrangements, and reserve two airline tickets to Cartagena for the next day, and a cabin on the next ship from Cartagena to New York. I responded to the telegram asking them to send the necessary papers to the American Consulate in Barranquilla, sponsoring our residence visas. Our wedding plans were carried out exactly as planned. The religious ceremony was held in the morning in the Iglesia de la Sagrada Pasion. My best man was the Argentine Ambassador, Mr. Ramon del Rio, and Lucía's godparents were her parents and Alfonso Hernandez. The reception took place at Lucía's home.

In the afternoon, we left from Techo Airport to Cartagena and stayed at the beach-front Hotel Caribe. A few days later we traveled to Barranquilla to get our visas and we stayed at the Hotel del Prado. With the sponsorship of IBM, our residence visas were granted almost immediately and we returned to Cartagena to await our ship. We boarded the Santa Paula with 36 suitcases and trunks. The cruise was excellent with all sorts of entertainment and even some time for meditation...

Everything was changing in my life: not only my

marital status, but also my office, my colleagues, the country where I lived and the language I spoke. What I would notice the most would be the change in my daily activities. Up until this point I had always been on the front line, serving our customers, until they were completely satisfied with our machines. At the end of an assignment, I would approach the manager to tell him that my daily presence was no longer needed as everything was now being handled smoothly by their own personnel. On many of those occasions I heard the "mermaid's call", to the tune of: "you must be well paid by IBM, but we will double your salary if you choose to stay with us". My loyalty towards IBM made it impossible for me to accept these offers, and while I always expressed my gratitude for their proposals, at the same time I assured them that they could always count on my assistance when necessary.

In the port of New York we were met by Mr. Califano and Mr. Rebsamen from IBM who took care of our luggage, as well as our friend Jaime Restrepo, who was in New York, representing the Colombian newspaper "El Tiempo".

CHAPTER FIVE

IN NEW YORK AGAIN

We arrived at the New Weston Hotel, and on the following day I went to my new office at 590 Madison Avenue, world headquarters for IBM. There I received a welcome letter from President Watson, who was traveling in Europe at the time. Later on I discovered confidentially that I had made a very good impression on Mr. Watson during the conventions in Rio de Janeiro and Buenaventura, and that he was the only person who could make the decision of assigning a foreigner to a post in the United States.

It took us two weeks to find a permanent home in New York City. We finally chose a small apartment in a residential hotel, the Dover, on Lexington Avenue and 57th Street, only two blocks from my office. I also purchased a car, a new Pontiac Catalina, which proved very useful in our travels and visits. We visited the Giraults almost every weekend in their home in Summit, New Jersey. They had three children, and as mentioned earlier, their daughter Marie-Claude was my Godchild. Our weekends in New Jersey didn't last long -- Raymond was transferred to Brazil to become General Manager there. We went to Endicott for more than a month so that I would have the opportunity to observe the typical IBM U.S. sales courses. This would help me to implement similar sales courses in Latin America, after making some important modifications. It was necessary to adapt the courses to our Latin American character:

one example where change was needed were the chants that started each class, praising IBM and its products. All of the students were recent graduates from the best colleges and universities. Some of them moved on from their sales training to great careers within the company. One example is John Opel, from the Class of 1062, who moved on to become President of IBM, many years after Mr. Watson's death.

Lucía enjoyed Endicott in spite of the fact that she spent her days alone. During the first few days we stayed in the Homestead, but later we moved to the Frederick Hotel in order to be closer to all of my classmates. From the beginning, it was clear to me that Lucía not only enjoyed being part of the IBM Family, but she was already fully adapted to it. After some quick driving lessons from me, she spent her days practicing her driving throughout the town even though she still didn't have her license. Shortly after that she took her road test and received her first Drivers License in Endicott, which allowed her to drive throughout the United States.

We returned to New York City and I had the privilege of working with Arthur Watson, youngest son of the President. He was his father's right hand man, in charge of all overseas operations. He spoke Spanish and French quite well, and I was the person in charge of Spanish speaking countries. Among other things, I supervised the translation of our machine manuals. We had three translation centers: one in Madrid, a second one in Mexico City and the third in Buenos Aires. I was always consulted when we needed to name a new machine part, in order to prevent confusion and use the same terminology throughout the organization. In this way, we created a situation in which our technicians in many different countries spoke the same language when they gathered at meetings. In spite of that, I was never able to get people in Spain to use the word "computer". To this day they still say "ordenador" in Spanish, rather than "computador"...

As our business in Latin America continued growing, Carlos Vidal managed South America from his office in Peru, and I managed Central America and the Caribbean from New York. I began my many travels in Cuba where I was able to see my old friend Marcial Digat, who acted as Manager there. After that I continued in Mexico, Guatemala, El Salvador, Honduras, Nicaragua, Costa Rica and Panama. Some of my trips were a month long or more. Costa Rica was the country that most impressed me with its liberal democracy. I will never forget the morning when sitting on a park bench in the main square in front of the Presidential Palace, I was having my shoes shined. Next to me was a distinguished looking man who was also getting his shoes shined. After he was done, he walked away and entered the Presidential Palace. I asked my shoe shine man if he knew the gentleman in question and he replied: "Yes, he is President Figueres, and he has his shoes shined here every morning before going to his office". During my travels I had the opportunity to meet the most important and influential people in each nation of my territory. I remember President Anastasio Somoza's invitations to "Montelimar" his great country home on the Pacific Ocean.

Upon my return to New York I wrote reports to Arthur Watson (we called each other by first name, Dick and Luis) about the state of affairs of our business in each country with my recommendations which were almost always followed, including transfers or removal of Managers. We once held a special class for our Latin American customers in Endicott. I spent the entire time with them, as many didn't speak English very well. Dick came to Endicott for the graduation banquet, and we had the chance to play a round of golf. Of course, Dick won...

We rented a beach house at Point Lookout and spent a wonderful summer there. A lot of our friends came to visit us there, some of them even from Colombia. Among them I remember the Herrera and Arensburg families. I also remember Alvaro, Lucía's brother who was studying at Valley Forge Military Academy. We purchased a small motor boat and used it for exploring the ocean and fishing. We enjoyed eating fresh fish. Lucía and I spent a few days in Montauk Point, a lovely place at the eastern tip of Long Island.

Meanwhile, Lucía was only two months away from delivering our first child and she was in the care of a famous obstetrician from New York Hospital. As our family was about to become larger, we moved to a larger apartment outside of Manhattan where the air is cleaner. My five-minute walk to the office became a one-hour commute from the north by car. But on the morning of October 13 of 1951 when Lucía went into labor, we made it to Manhattan in 30 minutes! Of course, I knew that the New York Police wouldn't stop me for speeding if I tied a handkerchief to the car antenna, which was the signal for this kind of emergency. We arrived at New York Hospital just in time, and at 10:00 am, our first daughter Joyce, was born. She was named after her godmother. My firstborn was beautiful and I was proud to have started our own family together with Lucía.

The IBM New York family made its presence known with flowers and gifts. Even Dick Watson came to the hospital to bring his gift to us personally. This is when Lucía started her collection of photo albums, and since an image is worth a thousand words, I use these old albums today to bring back memories from the old days as I write these memoirs.

My mother-in-law, Candelaria, came from Colombia to meet her first granddaughter and spend some time with us. Summer of 1952 was approaching and we left Joyce with her grandmother and uncle Alvaro, and Lucía and I went on a road trip all the way to California to spend our summer vacation. We went everywhere on a mad race against the clock: through Washington D.C.; Indianapolis, where I was allowed to race my own car at the famous race track, while Lucía watched from the stands; Saint Louis, the Grand Canyon, the Mojave Desert, where we had a tire blowout due to the heat and speed; Las Vegas, where we enjoyed gambling in all of the casinos; Los Angeles and Hollywood. There we saw my friend Atherton from IBM Class 1062, who had Twentieth Century Fox as one of his customers. He took us to spend an exciting day at the studios where they were shooting "Niagara" with Marilyn Monroe. We watched them film the scene where she is naked in a bathtub. After that we had lunch in the studio cafeteria where we dined among all the biggest stars of the day. This was no standard tourist tour of the studios; it was something very special...

Continuing our journey we spent time in San Francisco, then Salt Lake City, where we challenged what was left of our poor car in the salt fields; the Rocky Mountains, where we played with snow in spite of the heat; Chicago, and from there, a mad dash to make it home on the last weekend of our vacation. It was a race against time back to New York, where I had to be in my office on the following Monday morning.

The life of the founder of IBM was now in decline and he was much less active than in the past. He still kept his office, which encompassed the entire 17th floor. We saw him less as time passed, however, he was always present at social gatherings together with his wife. Shortly after we arrived in New York I recall a gift that Mrs. Watson gave to Lucía: a book entitled "Cooking for Two". At one of our social gatherings they met again, and Mrs. Watson, aware of our growing family, said "you are not cooking for two anymore, dear...!".

Mr. Watson could allow himself the luxury of being less active: in 1952 his eldest son, Thomas, was named President of IBM Corporation, and his youngest son, Arthur became General Manager of IBM World Trade. Naturally, the old gentleman kept his role as Chairman of the Board of Directors and was still in full command. Many might have thought of this as blatant nepotism, but we should always keep in mind that he had raised his sons to do this work very well. Most of the shareholders trusted these decisions and the stock value continued climbing...

The new generation was more confident in electronics than its predecessor. Remington Rand with its new "Univac" was taking the lead, and they had installed one of their machines in the Census Bureau, one of our oldest customers. Tom Jr. made some excellent business decisions, naming Lamotte and Williams as Executive Vice Presidents. IBM was a huge company now and it was necessary to delegate responsibilities. He placed none less than Vin Learson in charge of projects 701 and 702, whom I called the Giant because he was more than six feet tall. Two years later, we had more than twice as many of these machines installed or pending for installation, than there were Remington Rand

Univacs.

In the meantime, the elderly Mr. Watson was dedicated to assist his son Dick with the foreign company. IBM World Trade Corporation became independent and we moved to a building in front of the United Nations. Even though Mr. Watson had an office there with us, he still maintained his old office on the 17th floor at Madison Avenue. I continued traveling through my Central American territory, and in early 1953, Lucía traveled to Colombia to introduce our beautiful daughter Joyce to her relatives and to give birth to our second child. I was on a business trip in Panama, when on April 19th I received a telegram saying: "Here I am Daddy. Love, Junior". I traveled to Bogotá and met my first son, a beautiful blond child with blue eyes. We baptized him with my name, and for many years called him Junior. Lucía was in great health and we were all very happy. I had the opportunity to meet Lucía's grandmother, Mrs. Maria Jesus Uribe Arango de la Sierra, a respectable matriarch from Antioquia, who was nearly one hundred years old. She had 18 children in her youth! Another tropical miracle...

We returned to New York with a fantastic Colombian nanny called Monica. Since the apartment was now too small for us, we began house hunting. We bought one in a very nice location, Beacon Hill Road in Port Washington. It was near the Long Island Sound and close to the IBM Country Club for company employees. There we were able to play golf and other sports. It took me one hour on the train to get to work everyday. We also traded our Pontiac Catalina for a large station wagon, where we could fit the family, the stroller and all of the equipment required for two small children.

In my travels through Central America I met many

important people, including three presidents who were all assassinated in the same year: Remon of Panama, Castillo Armas from Guatemala and Somoza from Nicaragua. In 1954 Dick Watson was named President of IBM World Trade, which under the guidance of his father had grown at a quicker pace than the American organization. The IBM family continued growing, and so did my own. On April 18 of the same year my daughter Karen was born at North Shore Hospital. I had a big argument with Dr. Mellow, who delivered her. Just a few hours before her birth on Easter Sunday, he told me that she was going to be born feet first. He calmed me down telling me that there was no danger, and told me to go on to Mass, and come back to see my newest miracle.

The well-known saying of being "born on your feet" is almost the same as falling feet first, as cats always do. The few people who are born this way are very special people. Ever since she was a small child, Karen was always brave and adventurous. Most homes in the United States don't have fences, and many times dogs from neighboring homes would come into our back yard when the children were there. Our older children would run away from the dogs, but Karen would always play with them. She would stick her fingers in the dogs' mouths, poke them in the eyes or pull on their ears, until they would get tired of it and run back home.

Lucía's father came from Colombia to spend some time with us. I took a vacation to spend some time with him and accompany him on visits to some factories that were related to his own business. We also went to Washington D.C. and to all of the nearby beaches. Monica, the nanny we brought from Colombia, turned out to be excellent and became a real member of the family. Not only were we able to leave her alone with the children, but she was also a great help to Lucía, as she took care of all of the housekeeping chores.

The following year, on April 3, 1955, our daughter Denise was born at North Shore Hospital. She weighed more than nine pounds and was delivered by Dr. Teta. Denise was a beautiful, chubby baby, who loved to eat and only cried when she was hungry. Around that same time, Carlos, Lucía's brother, arrived on a Colombian ship. Carlos was a cadet in the Cartagena Naval Academy.

In IBM we continued setting the pace. We presented the 608, which was the first transistorized computer. Shortly thereafter we were shocked when our competitor Remington Rand joined forces with Sperry Corporation and became Sperry Rand, a company even larger than IBM. When we had important visitors who did not speak English, Dick Watson always asked me to make our equipment demonstrations in Spanish. We went to 590 Madison together to meet with Castillo Armas, President of Guatemala, and after the demonstration we offered a tea reception in his honor. On some of my last trips to Mexico and Central America I was accompanied by Tom Kirkland, vice-president of IBM World Trade. Tom didn't speak Spanish and I was the one in charge of the speech and presentation of a new movie about IBM. Sometimes I combined my travels with a convention, and I remember one in Panama that I attended together with Carlos Vidal.

In early 1956 I met in New York with Anastasio (Tachito) Somoza, son of the former President of Nicaragua, who had been assassinated. I invited him to lunch in the United Nations Delegates' Restaurant. In our conversation he mentioned that he was very interested in meeting our founder Mr. Watson, and asked if I could possibly arrange a meeting. Even though Mr. Watson rarely went to his office on the 17th floor of 590 Madison, I managed to arrange a meeting there. I went with Somoza to the office, and we sat by the desk of our venerable leader, and had a lengthy conversation with him. We spoke on varied subjects and Tachito invited him to visit Nicaragua. Mr. Watson said it would be difficult because he never traveled by plane. Somoza told him not to worry, and offered to send one of the many ships from his own Mamenic Cruise Line to the Port of New York, so that Mr. Watson could sail down to Nicaragua with his family and entire entourage...

Not much later, in June of the same year, Mr. Watson passed away. It was a major event in the world of business. President Eisenhower issued a statement to the press stating that "he had lost a great friend, and the country had lost a great citizen". Lucía and I attended his funeral at Brick Presbyterian Church on Park Avenue. There was a crowd of people on the street who were unable to enter the Church. The Church Minister was a great friend of the deceased, and his words of admiration were so eloquent and sentimental, that I shall never forget them. Mr. Watson's was buried at Sleepy Hollow Cemetery.

I lost my great teacher at IBM. From him I learned all of the best skills I used in my business life.

Regarding my friend Anastasio (Tachito) Somoza, shortly thereafter he was elected President of Nicaragua. I had told him once that there was a year in which I had shaken the hands of three Presidents, and all three had been assassinated in the same year. He replied: "well Luis, from now on I will never shake your hand, just in case". Tachito was in power for many years, and was finally toppled by the

Sandinista Revolution. He sought refuge in Paraguay, and two years later was assassinated...

At this point, I had lived in the United States continuously for five years, but I hadn't made an attempt to become an American citizen and began to feel some pressure to do so. After all, I was not only familiar with many IBM trade secrets, but also those of important customers, such as the Pentagon and our Military Products factory. I thought about this very carefully, and finally made a decision based on the fact that most of my children were American born and I planned to spend the rest of my life with them in the United States. My great friend Tom Fay, who was then Manager of Engineering and also my golf partner at the IBM Country Club in Port Washington, congratulated me and offered to be my godfather in the process of adopting my new nationality.

Raymond had returned from Brazil, and we were once again working together in New York. In that same year of 1956, IBM decided to open operations in Ireland, and they sent him there as General Manager. Everything you see today in IBM Ireland is there thanks to Raymond. When he arrived in Dublin, IBM Ireland was just Raymond, and his briefcase in a hotel room. On December 29th of this year, my family grew once again with the arrival of my son Pierre in Nassau Hospital, weighing 8 pounds, 5 ounces. He was a beautiful and strong baby. Lucía insisted on naming him Pierre, because she felt our French family name required a French first name. She also said that even though she did all of the work, our children all looked like me!

I was so busy with my office duties that I didn't always have time to know the details of all of our visitors from other countries. One day I ran into someone in the hall, and he was very shocked when I didn't know who he was. How could that be possible, when he was no less than Jacques Maisonrouge from IBM France who had been in New York for several days! He insinuated that not only I, but also IBM New York did not work very well at all. He seemed like a modern day La Fayette to me. I mention this incident because many years later it brought repercussions that I will speak about in a later chapter.

The two sons, now working without the wise guidance of the "Old Gentleman", managed IBM on their own. Tom was in charge of the American Company and Dick was in charge of IBM World Trade. I knew them both well. Tom was a solid man, who had been shaped by all of the struggles and battles he had fought with his father throughout his life. His father tried to model him in his own image, and they even had the same name! I believe the only rest Tom ever had was during the war, when he was piloting planes to Russia. There he excelled at something he really enjoyed, and something that his father feared and hated. On the other hand, Dick was the young boy of the family, who was led by his father's hand almost until the day of his death. He adored and respected his father, and always tried to prevent his anger. Many times he said to me: "Luis let's remove that Personal and Confidential letter from my father's desk and take care of this problem ourselves". They were usually letters from another country, where someone felt that they were being treated unfairly. These were all human relations' matters that we could resolve easily without the need of irritating our big boss, who was already in poor health.

Our staff continued growing, and we continued to announce new transistorized electronic products. We had already resolved our monopoly lawsuit with the American government.   After several years of litigation, we finally reached an agreement whereby we now had to rent or sell our products.   I would say that this was beneficial for us because it gave us two different ways to negotiate with our customers.   The proof of this is that we grew at a pace never seen before...

When we were in our office facing the United Nations Building, Dick asked me if I would agree to return to Colombia as General Manager.   Things were not going well there, the staff was unhappy and they were threatening to organize a union.   I would be going there to put out a fire.   After many years of progress under the management of Alberto Laverde, the company was now in the hands of Guido Forgnoni, who was called back to New York soon after.

CHAPTER SIX

IN COLOMBIA AGAIN

I arrived in Bogotá the first week of 1958. A short time later Dick arrived in the company airplane in order to officiate my taking possession as general manager. We convened all the personnel in the main conference room of the Hotel Tequendama. He made an effort to introduce me in Spanish, although this was not really necessary since most of the older employees already knew me. Also present was Carlos Vidal.

On my first day at work at my new office, I walked from the Hotel Tequendama. Even though it was eight o'clock in the morning, which was the normal start time for the office personnel, I found the work area nearly empty. Since IBM manufactured employee time clocks, I asked the receptionist for the employee time card holder. She informed me that in Colombia, IBM managers do not punch time cards. Nevertheless, I prompted her to add a card with my name on it, and informed her that I would be punching in and out daily. One half-hour later, I called the sales manager in order to request some documents. His secretary informed me that he had not yet arrived, so I told her to have him call me as soon as he arrived. I made the same request to the accounting manager and other section managers, all with the same results.

One hour later, the people I had called began to arrive in my office. As we drank a cup of coffee and they gave me the information that I needed to send to New York, most of them had the same excuse: "The traffic this morning was terrible." Almost all of the days that followed I used the same tactic, but I never confronted them about arriving late for work. Since good habits are spread through example, I continued to punch-in with my time card every morning at eight o'clock. This, along with early morning chats, which included information requests, had all the office managers punching in with their cards at the correct time within two weeks time.

For me it was a pleasure returning to my old stomping grounds, and again having Miss Meier as my English-speaking secretary. Some of the employees were in the process of making official a labor union with the Ministry of Labor. Our company had relocated from the site it occupied when I had left in 1950. It was now located on Calle 22, adjacent to the Teatro Faenza. The facilities were inadequate and the neighborhood was somewhat precarious. I assigned myself two very important tasks: Move our office to a better location and interview each employee. I found the location almost immediately. Monsignor Salcedo of the "Accion Cultural Popular" facilitated a building, whose construction was being completed, on the corner of the Avenida Decima and Calle Veinte. It even had an activities room that could be used when necessary. The Monsignor offered to name it the "IBM Building" if that was desired. Following our company's policies, I declined the generous offer.

In my new office, over a cup of coffee, one by one, I continued dialoging with all the discontent employees. Sometimes there were personal problems that I would immediately resolve. I had learned quite a bit about human relations working along side the Boss in New York. I discovered many injustices, so the first thing I did was implement an "open door" policy which stated: "If you have a problem, ask your immediate superior to help you resolve it. If he cannot help you, come to my door and I will solve it for you."

In the meantime, I had been having an ongoing dialogue with our lawyer, Hernando Castilla Samper, who had succeeded his late Uncle, Juan Samper. In the past, Juan had been a great friend and confidant. We played golf in the Country Club. He had been given the charge of drawing up the company statutes, and had a major role in the founding of IBM in Colombia. His nephew Hernando was also a close friend of mine when we were both bachelors. I filled Hernando in on our personnel problem, and asked him if his intervention in this labor issue was necessary. The Ministry of Labor had received a letter of intent with its required twenty five signatures from IBM employees. Their intention was to form a labor union. He informed me that I was doing fine without his or any other legal intervention. A few days later I called to let him know that I had met with five union delegates who had informed me: "Don Luis, we have withdrawn our intent to form a labor union with the Ministry of Labor..."

And my real family? Just fine, thank you! We rented a large house, which we later bought, in a residential neighborhood. Lucía was happy to be near her family again. Our five children: Joyce our oldest entered the first grade in the "Colegio Nueva Granada," and the younger ones went to a nearby preschool. We had three maids and a good chauffeur named Reinaldo, who drove our new Oldsmobile. Our social life grew rapidly. We were members of the Country Club, and while I played a round of Golf, the children would take swimming lessons. They had never had the illnesses that children usually get in Colombia, so suddenly they all became ill with all sorts of bugs including the chicken pox. Another thing that was a let down for the children was that back in the United States, whenever they abandoned their toys or bicycles in front of our house, they could return the next day and find everything as they had left it. But here, their things would disappear like magic...

Even though I had sworn that I would never drive in any more automobile races, I could not resist when I received a call from the Automobile Club. They had organized a race on the landing strips of the new "Eldorado" airport on the Sunday before its inauguration. I entered the race with my Oldsmobile, which had a "rocket" engine, and while being cheered on by Lucía and the children, I won the race. The year flew by and the family was going to get bigger. We celebrated Christmas Eve with all of Lucía's family, and early Christmas morning we drove to the "Clinica Palermo," where our daughter Michele was born. She always remarks that life has cheated her since her brothers and sisters all celebrate and receive gifts twice a year, on their birthdays and on Christmas, while she only receives gifts once a year, on her birthday: Christmas Day...

IBM of Colombia continued to grow. We built our new factory in Bogotá, where punch cards were produced and electric typewriters were assembled. These typewriters were sold in Colombia and exported to neighboring countries. In the factory we had a magnificent cafeteria which most of our employees got in the habit of using instead of going home for lunch, thus saving themselves more than an hour of travel time. I made it a point to have lunch with our factory workers one day per week. This fraternization contributed to our human relations.

Around those days I completed twenty-five years of

continuous work with IBM. All the other IBM countries had a "Quarter Century Club." IBM of Colombia did not have one, since none of its employees had achieved this milestone. Because of this, the club was inaugurated with me. I was surprised with a big banquet, which was held in the main ballroom of the Hotel Tequendama. Since there were no other local members but me, all the company personnel attended. Among them was a graphic artist, who used his creative prowess to drape the walls with caricatures depicting me in all the activities I had labored in up until that day. In the end there were the speeches, and then I was presented with the famous gold watch, an IBM tradition.

1959 began with an IBM South American convention in Chile. Lucía accompanied me, and when the convention ended, we traveled to Argentina where Benito Esmerode put a company car at our disposal. We drove to La Plata, and spent three days in Mar del Plata. In Buenos Aires we stayed at the Plaza Hotel. Here we visited my sister Aida; a widow with two adult sons. Aida and her older son have since died. Her other son Alberto is still alive. Justo Del Carril invited us to have lunch. He gave Lucía some jewelry that had belonged to my late Aunt Cirila. We also visited Montevideo, Viña del Mar, Lima and Quito.

Upon my return to Bogotá, in addition to attending to my obligations with IBM, I did not ignore my civic activities. I was elected President of the Colombian-American Chamber of Commerce, founded and was first President of the Systems and Procedures Association, was founding member of the Board of "Diriventas," became a member of the Board of Directors of the "Accion Cultural Popular," "Incolda" and The Rotary Club. My peers in these activities were important businessmen. Among them I remember

Hernan Echevarria Olozaga. We would get up very early in the morning and have a working breakfast in one of our homes. Around that time there was a lot of publicity in the press regarding my promotion to President-General Manager of IBM of Colombia.

We rented a large "finca" (vacation house) named "Catay" in Villeta; a small town outside Bogotá. It had a swimming pool and the property was traversed by the railroad. During school vacations, the whole family would live here in what was appropriately called the "hot country." Located close by were the "fincas" belonging to friends. One of them was the finca "Potosi," were we would meet up with Jaime Restrepo, his wife Elvira Samper and their four daughters. In Catay, which was located two hours from Bogotá, I would spend the weekends. On Mondays, I would leave very early in the morning in order to return to my labors in Bogotá. When the children returned to school, we would spend the weekends in Villeta. To celebrate our tenth wedding anniversary, we had a grand party there. It started on a Saturday with lunch and ended early Sunday morning. We had one hundred guests and "Los Isleños" band supplied the music.

We had outgrown our house in Bogotá, so we bought a larger one to the north of the city. It sat on about four acres of land, and was named "Rancho Grande." It was ideal for the children. They even had a pet donkey named "Manuela." There was another smaller house located on the property where I allowed Reinaldo, our chauffeur, to live with his wife and six children. On school days, very early in the morning, all the children would pile into our station wagon, and he would drive them to school. At this point, all of my older children attended the English-speaking "Colegio

Nueva Granada." School officials informed me that I had set a precedent in the school by having my five children enrolled concurrently. Because of this rarity, I was given a tuition discount for the fourth and fifth child. Since this was a lay school, our eldest children prepared themselves for their First Holy Communion in different churches. Joyce received hers in 1959, and Luis his in 1960. Since our residence was located so close to the back gate of the Country Club, I was given the key to its lock thus facilitating our access to it.

Klaus Hendricks was named the General Manager for IBM of South America, with his office in Uruguay. One of the reasons for my mission in Colombia was to find and prepare an individual that would replace me as General Manager, when I eventually returned to New York. This task was not an easy one and it took some time. I would visit our branch offices and would personally observe the performance of each one of our managers. This way I could choose from a pool of candidates at a national level. In 1960, in order to get a more accurate evaluation of a candidate's performance in my absence, I chose to take my vacation time in the United States.

Lucía and I took a plane to Miami where we spent a few days. We stayed at the Hotel Fontainebleau. In Miami we visited Alberto and Magolita Laverde, who were living there at the time. Together we went to see the "Miss USA" Beauty Pageant. In New York, we stayed at the Summit Hotel. I took the opportunity to visit the IBM office, where I made a personal report on our operations in Colombia, and got updated on activities in New York. We went to the theater and got "caught up" with the latest Broadway shows. We also visited old friends, among them the Pardos, and Tom and Signa Fay. Lucía enjoyed shopping immensely, which included gifts for her, the family and friends.

Our return home was by sea. We took a ship directly back to the port of La Guaira in Venezuela. We stayed a few days in Caracas, where we saw my old friend Fernandez Mira who had a diplomatic post there and had married "Bibi".

Anew in Bogotá, IBM was in a flurry of activity with the installation of new electronic equipment. We installed, for the first time in Colombia, two 650's. One in "Coltejer" and the other one in "Bavaria." In addition, we signed a contract to install a 1401 for the Department of Public Works of Medellin. Meanwhile, since things were back to normal and IBM was prospering in Colombia, the time came for my return to New York, and the naming of a new General Manager for IBM of Colombia. Klaus Hendricks came up from Montevideo and decided that my replacement would be Carlos Salgado.

I made a short trip to New York in order to prepare for the return of my whole family. As always, Mr. Califano was of great assistance. Keeping in mind that our office was located in the United Nations Plaza, it was very convenient for me to use the Grand Central Station train terminal which was only a few minutes walking distance. I also had to choose a location with good schools for our children. It was also more practical to temporarily install ourselves in a hotel located in the general area chosen to live, which I decided was to be to the north of the big city. After some intensive research, we made reservations in The Hotel "Gramatan" which was located in the city of Bronxville. I enrolled my five older children in the local public elementary school. They were scheduled to begin classes on the day following our arrival.

I returned to Colombia to find Lucía distressed about

106

the fact that she was going to leave her home where she had spent four delightful years with her family close at hand. But when I informed her about the arrangements that I had made, she accepted it like a loyal "IBM wife".

Just like he had manifested to me, Dick Watson arrived with his wife Nancy in Bogotá. I had a special surprise prepared for Dick; I had developed a good friendship with the President of the Republic, Alberto Lleras Camargo. Even though I had known him for a number of years, I was able to strengthen our friendship, when after his last State visit to the United States, I presented President Lleras with a souvenir book dedicated by IBM at the Presidential Palace. This keepsake described all the details and activities of his official visit to the United States.

I made the suggestion that Dick should be conferred with the "Cruz de Boyaca" as a result of all the contributions that IBM had made to education in Colombia. This was the maximum Government bestowed medal of honor that could be received by any person in The Republic of Colombia. Dick's father had already been honored with this medal several years back. One day after Dick's arrival, accompanied by the United States Ambassador, we went to the Presidential Palace where we were received by President Lleras, who personally presented him with the "Cruz de Boyaca." Later, Dick, his wife and the Ambassador joined me for lunch at my home in order to celebrate this event. Dick was so amazed with "Manuela" the donkey, and considering that he also had young children, I offered it to him as a gift. We later thought about the logistics of shipping the animal and quickly forgot about the matter.

The main function was a banquet in one of the large event rooms of the "Club Militar." Dick gave the main speech, in which he gave a background of the progress that IBM had made in Colombia under my watch, and his hopes that it would continue growing at this pace. Again, we were going to distance ourselves from Colombia; Lucía was going to miss her family and childhood friends, as I would miss all my old friends too. I had many people who collaborated with me in IBM of Colombia, who despite the many years that have passed I still remember. Among them, Gonzalo Janer, Enrique Rugeles, Alvaro Aguirre, Miss Margaret Meier, and many others...

We sold the two cars, and since we did not have time to sell the house, the company lawyers took charge of this matter. While the movers were preparing to pack our furniture and other belongings, we went to live in the Hotel Tequendama. We were set up in a grand suite with two adjacent bedrooms. In the mornings, the children were picked up in front of the hotel by the school bus of the Colegio Nueva Granada. This way, they would miss only one day of school; the day of travel to the United States. Just before initiating our return, I gathered all the children, who were a happy group, and told them that "tomorrow we return to the United States. There you will not have a chauffeur; your mother will take care of that. You will have to shine your own shoes and take care of other small chores, since we are leaving behind all the people that were at our service. We will only take Blanca." After this speech I asked them: "Do you still want to go?" They all responded in unison with a big "YESSSSS!" When the time came to pay the hotel bill there was a strange added charge: "Paint and labor to repaint walls". My children had kept themselves busy drawing murals and graffiti.

Madrid 1940 - Inauguration of the course with my students. At my left is the General Manager of IBM in Spain, Mr. Fernando de Asua. (L. Lamassonne, seated far left).

1941 - Farewell lunch given by IBM Spain. (L. Lamassonne, seated far right).

1944 - In Medellin - dictating correspondence to Alberto Quiroga.

1948 - In New York - Receiving from Mr. Wilson my Hundred Percent Club certificate.

March, 1950 - In Buenaventura - Mr. Thomas Watson, commending me on my work. To our left is Alberto Laverde and to our right Carlos Vidal taking notes.

March, 1950 - Mr. Watson with the employees of IBM of Colombia.

August, 1950 - Our arrival in New York on the "Santa Paula". We were met by Messrs. Rebsamen and Califano, IBM executives.

1950 - Our famous 1062 class in Endicott.

THOS. J. WATSON
590 MADISON AVENUE
NEW YORK 22, N.Y.

Paris, France
September 13, 1950.

Dear Mr. Lamassonne:

Thank you very much for your nice note to Mrs. Watson and me. We are very pleased about your marriage and wish for you and your bride every happiness for the future. I know that she is a very fine young lady and both Mrs. Watson and I are looking forward to meeting her after our return to the States.

We have had a very interesting and constructive trip to Europe. We met with our IBM organizations in England, Norway, Sweden, Denmark, Holland, Belgium, Luxembourg, Switzerland, Italy and France. We also had the pleasure of meeting IBM representatives from Finland, Germany, Spain, Portugal, Greece and Turkey at different places on our itinerary.

We shall sail for home late in the month and we look forward to seeing you on our return and personally welcoming you to World Headquarters.

Meanwhile Mrs. Watson and I send to you and Mrs. Lamassonne our best personal wishes and kindest regards.

Sincerely yours,

Mr. Luis A. Lamassonne
20 East 57th Street
New York City 22,
N.Y.

Letter from the founder of IBM, Mr. T. J. Watson.

113

Mexico 1952 - Cutting the ribbon at the inauguration of our offices in Guadalajara.

1954 in Cuba - Giving Nicanor Infiesta his Hundred Percent Club pin. Observing is the General Manager of IBM Cuba, Mr. Marcial Digat and his wife Anita.

1955 - 590 Madison Ave. New York - Doing a demonstration of our equipment to the President of Guatemala, Coronel Castillo Armas. At the extreme right is Dick Watson.

1956 - with Mr. T. J. Watson, "Tachito Somoza" and Tom Kirkland. Mr. Watson passed away a few months later.

December 1958 in Colombia - Miss Margaret Meier is giving Lucía a gift during my "Quarter Century Club" party, celebrated at the Tequendama Hotel. On the left is Alejandro Castilla Samper, IBM's attorney.

Bogotá 1962 - With the President of Colombia, Alberto Lleras Camargo and Dick Watson, the day that the President bestowed on him the "Cruz de Boyaca" in the Presidential Palace.

116

January 31, 1962 - At the airport in Bogotá, on our way back to New York with the whole family.

August, 1963 - My son Luis observing with great interest our powerful computer, also present are some customers from Latin America.

Poughkeepsie 1964 - My daughter Joyce is also very attentive to the demonstration being made of our system 7010, with some customers from Bolivia.

New York 1966 - Lunch offered by the Colombian American Chamber of Commerce to German Arciniegas (left) who is talking with Alberto Lleras Camargo (right).

New York 1966 - Receiving from Chancellor German Zea the "Order of San Carlos". Observing are my wife Lucía and the President of Colombia, Ospina Perez.

Merry Christmas Happy New Year!
the Lamassonne's

12143 Hilltop Drive
Los Altos Hills, California   December 1969

Christmas card that we sent to our friends in 1969, depicting our move from New York to San Francisco. The picture was drawn by our daughter Karen.

119

CHAPTER SEVEN

IN NEW YORK AGAIN

Our return trip to New York had two additions: Michele, our daughter and Blanca, the maid, whom we brought from Colombia. We all stayed in the Hotel Gramatan. Our family added a lot of life to that hotel which was inhabited by mostly quiet adults. While the children were in school, Lucía and I were busy looking for a large house in the surrounding towns. We finally bought a house in the city of Larchmont located in Westchester County. The address was 7 France Place. Larchmont had excellent schools and was bordered by the Long Island Sound. The house was constructed of stone and brick, English style. It had seven bedrooms and seven bathrooms.

The children attended a Catholic school, Saints John and Paul School. In May of 1962, in the church of that same school, Karen and Denise received their First Holy Communion. We became members of the "Orienta Beach Club." It had a large sandy beach and the children really enjoyed it. We would take out small boats and go fishing and sailing. Lucía and I played Bridge. The train station was a very short distance from our new home. I would walk to the station in the mornings and ride the train into the city. While I read the New York Times, the train would arrive in Grand Central Station, only a few minutes walk from my office.

I became a part of the international sales office, which was directed by Niky Hauser. Our job was to prepare an agenda for important customers that were sent to us from our offices in foreign countries. Sometimes they did not speak any English, so we would become their interpreters. We had access to almost all the local social clubs, and our secretaries would take charge of making reservations for luncheons and other activities. Speaking of secretaries, I was extremely delighted to have Anne Marie Stigler as the head Secretary. I had known her for a number of years, and had conducted her first interview to see if her Spanish was adequate enough for her to work for IBM. At our disposal were the best limousines of the city. The drivers were well educated and very professional. Our sales team was conformed of employees of different races who came from different countries. Their job was to tend to our important customer's needs. Generally, these customers were managers, or presidents of companies, who would come to the United States for a short time in order to conduct their business. We would open the doors of similar local customers, in order that these visitors could apprise themselves of the performance of our hardware in an application similar to their own business. Sometimes we would prepare a conference for them with a demonstration, and would almost always add the finishing touch to their tour by taking them to our production plant in Poughkeepsie, which was our biggest and most modern plant. Here we assembled and produced our biggest computers. It was located two hours north of the city, via a beautiful flower and tree-lined highway.

If our visitor was a scientist, we would also give him a tour of our "T.J. Watson Scientific Lab," which was located nearby and in which we employed two Nobel Prize recipients. We would have lunch at the plant and in the evening, on our drive back to the city, since my home was located on the way, I would invite our visitors to my residence so they could meet my family and have a drink. This personal touch was greatly appreciated, especially by first time visitors to this country. This gave them an opportunity to see how we lived here.

When I returned from Colombia, Dick Watson told me that I should continue doing public relations for IBM. He let me know that I could take all the time necessary in order to conduct this civic activity. He delegated some of these activities that he himself was conducting to me, especially the ones concerning Latin America. Since my name was now representing IBM in these organizations, I was showered with invitations to attend luncheons and all types of ceremonies. In a short time, once I became well known, I was elected as a member in various Boards of Directors.

Without overlooking my job responsibilities with IBM, I belonged to the Boards of Directors of: The Colombian-American Chamber of Commerce, The Inter-American Literacy Foundation, The Bolivarian Society of The United States, etc... Since I was very knowledgeable about Colombia, in one of the assemblies I was elected president of the Colombian American Chamber of Commerce and was subsequently re-elected to that same office for six consecutive years. Even though I had a secretary in this association whose name was Mr. Leclair, I had to organize a monthly luncheon honoring a Colombian dignitary. These luncheons would take place in the Waldorf Astoria or in other comparable hotels. The honored VIP would be an ex President, a new ambassador, a visiting Minister, etc. I would fill a conference room with bankers and New York businessmen who were somehow connected with The Republic of Colombia. Here they listened to the guest speaker, who I introduced both in English and Spanish, since in the auditorium there were individuals who did not understand one of the two languages.

Among some of the visiting dignitaries, I remember Alberto Lleras Camargo, Ex-President of Colombia and Secretary General of the OAS (Organization of American States), Misael Pastrana Borrero, who at the time was ambassador in Washington, and who was startled when in my introductory speech, I presented him as "the future President of Colombia." Mr. Pastrana jokingly commented "You seem to be nominating me for the Presidency of the Republic." Knowing the present political situation in Colombia, I answered him with an emphatic yes. A short time later, Mr. Pastrana returned to Colombia, was nominated as the candidate for the Conservative Party and won the presidential election against General Rojas Pinilla. He served a full 4-year term as President.

The validity of that election was questioned in Colombia. The President at the time was Carlos Lleras Restrepo, a very good leader who in a swift move had to institute Martial Law, which lasted some time. While still in office, President Lleras visited the United States. He was well received by the government in Washington. In New York, The Ambassador to the United Nations was Mr. Julio Cesar Turbay (who later was elected president of Colombia) and the minister plenipotentiary was Pedro Olarte, both friends of mine. I took great pleasure helping them organize the welcoming activities for President Lleras's visit to New York. There were two large dinners held in honor of the President and his wife. One was held at the Commodore Hotel, and was attended by many of the Colombians living in New York. The other dinner was a very elegant occasion and was held at the Plaza

Hotel, which I had the honor of presiding over as President of the Chamber of Commerce. At the main table, seated next to me was President Lleras, and next to Lucía, was his wife. As always, I ended my speech by offering a toast with our champagne glasses to the President, and to Colombia. President Lleras finished his speech by offering a toast to the President of The United States.

The computer business had such an enormous future that the world´s biggest companies ventured in to stake their claim. In the United States, General Electric and RCA, both many times larger than IBM, as other European and Japanese companies, suddenly became our competitors. As a result, my job was becoming more global. Not only did I have to keep track of our competitors' activities in the United States, but the rest of the world as well, which is where our visitors were coming from. For example: Our laboratory in Holland announced the "Reader-Sorter 1219," and the "Magnetic Character Reader 1419"---In Germany, at the Dusseldorf Data Center, the first IBM-7090 was installed---In the United States, IBM introduced the 7040 and 7044---In Europe, the first great "Univac 3" was installed---In Colombia the first IBM-1410 was installed for our customer "Intercol"---In Argentina, the first two "Univac-SS90" were installed for the National Railroad---In Colombia, the Medellin Department of Public Works had an IBM-1401 installed---In England, at the University of Manchester the first Ferranti "Atlas" was installed---The "Elliot Automation" company opened a production plant in Australia---Ray Fentriss was named Regional Manager for South America---Fernando Rodriguez was named General Manager in Mexico---In England, IBM installed the first "Stretch" super computer at the Office of Atomic Energy. (With this giant monster we almost lost our shirts)---The French Company Bull introduced the new Magnetic Character Code CMC-7 along with an RCA-301, under the name "Gamma-30"---Honeywell introduced its H-1800 computer---Borroughs introduced its "P-703 with CMC-7"---Elliot Automation presented its "Arch" line of computers for control of industrial processes---In Sweden, Saab, the aircraft manufacturer, entered the field with its D-21 System---Olivetti of Italy inaugurated a factory that produced high speed printers---IBM announced the 1440 Computer.---In France, the society of Mathematical Studies ordered the first "CDC-600"---The small "Univac-1004" was demonstrated in the Hanover Fair... Just to think, I had witnessed the birth of the first computers, which were then called electronic brains. They had vacuum tubes, took up a lot of space, would overheat and burn out, thus requiring huge amounts of air-conditioning. Now, in the age of the transistor, IBM and its competitors were coming up with new marvels almost daily...

In the summer of 1963 Lucía and I took a vacation to Europe. We started in Ireland, where my old friend Raymond Girault was General Manager of IBM of Ireland. He had arrived there a few years before to form the company, which now was a flourishing organization. We where in Dublin several days where we enjoyed its lush, green countryside along with Raymond, his wife Joyce and their three children.

Our vacation lasted almost a month. We continued on to London, Amsterdam, The Hague, Brussels, Luxemburg, Germany, and Switzerland. In Italy we visited various cities: Milan, Venice, Rome (where at the time a new Pope was being elected), Florence, Naples, Capri, Pisa, Amalfi, Portofino, Sorrento, Siena, and Pavia, where we visited my

Mother's relatives. On we went to Nice, Montecarlo, Paris, and San Jean de Luz, where we again met up with the Girault family, who had come over from Dublin to spend the summer in a house they owned there. Finally, Madrid, where we stayed at the Hotel Palace. Here we paid a visit to my old friend The Marquis of Ugena and his family. We also caught up with some of the members of my old Madrid "gang."

We returned to our home, very happy to see our children who were very well behaved during our absence. I continued with my routine at IBM. Dick Watson was elected President of the Board of Directors of IBM World Trade, and G.E. Jones President of the company. ---IBM announced the 7740 Communications Control System---The 1050 Data Communications System and the 1460 that could print eleven hundred lines per minute---Remington Rand shipped the first Thin Filmed Memory "Univac" to Germany---ICT acquired the Ferranti Computers Division and began to market the Atlas-1 and the Atlas-2---IBM inaugurated The Educational Center in Cuernavaca, Mexico---Electrologic introduced the ELX8 Computer---IBM inaugurated the Gaude Laboratory in France---In England, Leo Computers and English Electric merged to form English Electric-Leo Computers---IBM introduced the 6400---Honeywell announced the 1400---Philips of Holland founded its computer division---Juan De Bona of IBM Spain was named General Manager for IBM in South America. (In 1941, Juan and I worked together in Madrid)---ICT and General Electric made an alliance to develop and produce the 1300 Series---Siemens of Germany introduced its second computer, the 3003---Borroughs presented its Data and Disc Communication System---At the Leipzig Fair in East Germany, the first computer manufactured in the communist block, the "Vebzeiss," was introduced---IBM presented its new Magnetic Reader/Sorter 1420 and the Optical Alpha Numeric Reader 1428---Control Data Corporation opened its first European plant in Holland---In Colombia, The National Cash Register installed a 315 in the Compañia Colombiana de Seguros.

1964, a year full of blessings, finally arrived. IBM made the most important announcement in its history! The System 360! It was baptized with this name because it covered a circumference of 360 degrees in applications. The cost of its creation was the largest spent by man up to this date. More than five hundred million dollars were spent on this project. A cost greater than the development of the Atomic Bomb! On April 7 of that year, the day of this announcement, IBM chartered an express train from Grand Central Station, to our plant in Poughkeepsie. On this train, among those invited, were two hundred members of the press. Simultaneously that same day, the news was announced with much fan-fare in sixty-three cities in the United States and fourteen countries around the world. Spearheading this campaign was Tom Watson. Those of us who were near him could readily see his overwhelming emotion. The responsibility was such that Tom named his brother Dick to be in charge of the System 360 production, and Vin Learson in charge of sales. Later on, we were to find out that Vin and Dick did not totally meet eye to eye. While sales were enormous, the production began to lag thus causing delivery delays. The first deliveries were completed almost a year later, but there was so much expectation, that most of our customers waited patiently for the product.

That same year my home was also blessed. Our family grew for the seventh time with the birth of our daughter

Anna. She was born smiling (even today she has an almost permanent smile on her face), assisted by Dr. Delaquilla, on April 24 in New Rochelle Hospital. The time of birth was ten o'clock at night and she weighed in at seven pounds, eight ounces. Lucía was well enough to come home three days later. All our children were very excited, since it had been many years since such an occurrence had happened in our family. For them it was like getting a new toy, and whoever would listen to them, would be told about their new "baby sister." We bought a new ten-seater station wagon. This was the exact passenger count needed whenever we would all ride together, including Blanca, our Colombian nanny. In June of that same year, Pierre received his First Holy Communion in the Church of Saints John and Paul, and Michele, who was now in Kindergarten, participated in a fashion show.

My marriage couldn't get any better! Running a household as large and exuberant as mine was almost as hard as governing the IBM. In the United States, a family comprised of seven children was a handsome and rare sight. I will always remember two of my neighbors who I would run into daily on our way to work. They would wish me a "good morning" with a smile that I was never able to interpret. I am not sure if this smile was one of pity or admiration. Nevertheless Lucía, oh Lucía! She was such a dedicated and loving mother to our children, even though the most important thing a young mother could have was missing; the advice and help from her own mother. With all the comings and goings of my work, I distanced her twice from this privilege. In spite of all that, Lucía was not only a good mother, but also a great wife. She never complained whenever I would embark on business trips that would leave her and the children alone, sometimes for up to a month. I would say good-bye to her and some of the children at the airport, and remember upon my return from one of those trips, greeting and kissing the youngest, that was less than a year old at the time. He did not recognize me and began to cry. But it was also what in our work jargon we referred to as a "loyal IBM wife." Such as the numerous times she would entertain a customer in our home, or when I would call her from my office to ask her to leave the children in Blanca's hands, and to come to Manhattan because I had invited a customer and his wife to dinner and the theater. This required her to drive the car about thirty miles across bridges and through tunnels during the evening rush hour. Moreover, she was and still is the woman of my life...

With the announcement of the IBM System 360, our competition turned up the heat. Almost immediately, General Electric and the Bull Company formalized a financial agreement. Japanese computer manufacturers became more active. Among them were Nippon Electric, Tokyo Shibaura Electric (TOSBAC), Fujitsu (FACOM), OKI Electric, Hitachi and a few others, who together were a near monopoly. This Japanese consortium had IBM of Japan nearly cornered. In Australia, a company by the name of "Australia Computers" was formed, which was an association between Electric-Leo-Marconi of England and Amalgamated Wireless. Univac began operating in various European countries with its remote controlled 1104 and 1107 models. Siemens and RCA signed a patent and sales agreement. In Italy, General Electric and Olivetti, teamed up to exploit the computer and peripheral equipment market. Univac introduced its Real time System 1050. All this activity did not intimidate IBM. While it furiously worked on the production of its system 360, it also developed its new audio technical support system named the "7700 Audio Response." We also inaugurated the Hursley Laboratory in England, immediately giving us a connection for technical interchange between Essones in France, and Poughkeepsie in the United States.

Much to the delight of all the IBM personnel, the value of IBM shares continued to rise. The option to buy shares at a discount was a benefit offered to all high level executives. In the process, many of them were becoming millionaires. This was also true of all the other employees, but on a smaller scale. IBM was one of the first corporations to adopt this stock ownership plan. For the large part, its employees owned the company! In the production plants, workers were not paid by the hour. Everyone received a monthly salary. In addition to full medical benefits, everyone had the privilege of investing ten percent of their salary in IBM shares, at a fifteen percent discount of the Wall Street quote. There were no commissions charged for these transactions. It was only logical to predict that these workers would produce quality products and service, since they owned the company. In addition, annual salary surveys of all the positions offered were conducted in the top ten corporations. IBM would then top them all. All this, along with its excellent human relations since its founding, resulted in IBM never having a labor union...

Although on a smaller scale in Latin America, IBM and its competitors were also expanding. Since it was my region, I had my finger on its pulse and could detect even the most minimal activity. Some examples: In Uruguay, the "Banco Comercial" ordered its first IBM System 360---ICT installed a system in the Credit Corporation of Jamaica---Rodrigo Herrera was named Manager of IBM in Venezuela--

-IBM Brazil began exporting punching machines and verifiers 024, 026 and 056, manufactured in its own plant---IBM installed its first system in The Dominican Republic---D.J. Howard was named Manager of IBM in Trinidad---Univac installed its first 1004 in The Dominican Republic---The "Compañia Telefonica de Uruguay" had a Bull 300 and a Gamma-10 installed---In Jamaica, R. Grant was named manager of Borroughs ---Fernando de Asua, son of my old friend the Manager of IBM in Spain, was designated Regional Manager of IBM in South America. It seemed as though Spain had rediscovered America! Could it be that there was a manpower crisis in IBM of Latin America, and we would no longer be able to continue with our founder's precepts of "locals employed in each country from the manager to the security guard"---In Medellin, "Confecciones Colombia" had a Univac-1004 installed---M. Bonnet was named President of Bull-General Electric in Argentina---Also in Argentina, English Electric-Leo-Marconi installed its first KDP-10 in the Bank of London, and "Bairesco de Argentina" had a Bourroughs-270 installed---Bull of Mexico opened a Card Punch plant.

1965 arrived, and with difficulty, IBM began to deliver its first System 360's. The delivery and installation of the hardware could not keep up with customer orders. We were experiencing an increase in customer visits from all over the world. Along with the product presentations and tours, we would offer them all kinds of entertainment. If they liked the theater, we always had tickets available to the current Broadway hits. If they came with their wives, Lucía would accompany us, and before or after the show, we would dine in the best restaurants of the theater district. For lunches, I preferred to take my guests to places like the Metropolitan

Club, the Hemisphere Club, or the Delegates' Restaurant in the United Nations' building. When the location of a plant tour was too distant, we would use air transport instead of limousines. Tours to the Endicott plant for example, would begin with a short helicopter ride from the heliport on the top of the Panam Building to the airport. We would then travel by airplane to our destination in less than an hour. The return would be done in the same manner. This allowed us to complete the tour on the same day.

The war with our competitors was increasing daily and was more intense than ever. All sides continued to introduce, sell, produce and install new lines and products. IBM introduced PL-1, a new programming language, which had more capability than Fortran and Algol---Philips introduced the PR-8000, the first general use calculator---IBM announced the 1130, designed for scientific applications---J. Forster was elected president of Sperry Rand (Univac)---Bull introduced to the market the medium sized CE-400 and the M-40 computer, for scientific applications---IBM announced the Digital 1800 computer---In London, the Leo-326, the newest and most powerful of this line was installed---Honeywell produced three more models of its 200 series-the 1200, 4200 and the 8200---In Italy, Olivetti-Bull merged with Olivetti-General Electric---CDC introduced the 6800, which executed twelve million instructions per second---In England, Scientific Furnishings launched its G-900 and 9250 computers into the market---Elliot National Cash announced its 4100---IBM opened a new plant in Montpellier, France---ICT installed its first 1900 computer in London---IBM of Germany built a new plant in Mainz, which was utilized for the production of the System 360---Borroughs introduced its System E-100 and B-300, with on-line terminals, for use in the banking industry---English Electric-Leo-Marconi also introduced its new line of products based on the "Spectra 70."

My old friend Marcial Digat, an expatriate from his native and beloved Cuba, continued to plunder from Fidel Castro's hands the best men that had once belonged to IBM in Cuba. As a Good Samaritan, Marcial traveled throughout Latin America, observing his ex coworkers who continued working and advancing within that great Latin American IBM family. He also oversaw several promotions such as J.M. Covelo's being named manager of IBM in Honduras, the naming of Eugenio Ojeda as the IBM representative in the Dominican Republic and Hugh Kramer's promotion to General Manager of IBM in Colombia, thereby replacing Carlos Salgado. When Marcial completed his human relations' mission south of the Rio Grande, I was extremely delighted when he was subsequently assigned to head our visitor's bureau and my promotion to Manager of Special Activities within that same organization. My office was located next to Marcial's, and whenever our schedules permitted, we would have lunch together in nearby restaurants. It never occurred to me back in 1941 when I met Marcial in Havana, that twenty-five years later we would be working together in New York...

Tom Watson, who was now Chairman of the Board and Chief Executive Officer of IBM, as his father was for many years, was leading the company to grow at a phenomenal rate, a level his father would never have dreamed of. The annual growth was thirty percent! IBM had now placed itself among the ten biggest companies in the United States. Under his command, Tom named Al Williams, a finance genius, as President and Vin Learson, who was a sales wizard, third in command.

Tom always regretted having mistakenly named his brother Dick to head the production of the System 360. This decision had been made in good faith, based on wanting to prolong the Watson dynasty with his younger brother. This behavior caused Dick to resent his brother. His depression and preoccupation with this was apparent. Adding to the injury, their mother died at the age of eighty-two, ten years after the death of their father. For both brothers, this was a heavy blow not only because they had lost their mother whom they adored, but she also had been their advisor, who throughout the years had interceded on their behalf whenever they opposed their father on business matters. The news of her death saddened everyone who knew her. She had been a grand lady and a great wife, who accompanied Mr. Watson on almost all his business trips throughout the world. From this point forward, Tom devoted himself with more zeal to the expansion of IBM, and Dick took refuge in IBM World Trade where he was still CEO and Chairman of the Board.

Throughout the world, IBM's competitors continued production at an accelerated pace. A Japanese computer industry statistic put Nippon Electric in first place in Japan with 966 system installations, followed by Tokyo Shibaura Electric (TOSBAC) with 684 installations. Fujitsu (FACOM) with 365 installations came in third place. These were followed by: OKI Electric with 297 installations, Hitachi with 231, Uchida Yoko (USAC) with 87 and Mitsubishi Electric with 35 installations---It was estimated that in Russia there existed 2,500 installed computers---In the United States, Univac introduced its new 9000 series, considered by its creators as the advent of the fourth generation of computers. (Our System 360 was considered a third generation computer)---Robert McDonald was named President of Sperry Rand (Univac)---In Paris, Bull-General Electric introduced the new Gamma-140 and 141---Philips acquired forty percent of the German company "Seimag," which entered the market with the Data-100 computer---In France, the "Alcatel-2412" for military and nuclear applications was introduced---Honeywell bought out Computer Control Corporation---Elliot-Automation presented its new series 920 computers---Borroughs launched its third generation of computers with the B-2500 and the B-3500. The IBM Board of Directors named Vin Learson as president of the company, thereby replacing Al Williams, who had wanted to retire for some time now.

Extraordinary things were also occurring in my home. In 1966 our daughter Michele received her First Holy Communion in the church of Saints John and Paul. She was very thin at the time and would complain on our insisting that she should eat more. That summer we also rented a cottage in Fire Island. It was a beautiful, primitive beach which lacked both electricity and telephone service. Something worth telling occurred here; one morning while I was sitting on the beach reading, I observed that our children, accompanied by our maid Blanca, had gone swimming in the ocean. Almost immediately I heard the cries for help and could see someone's arms waving frantically for their life. I took off running in search of those agitated arms that were struggling not to sink. After an exhausting effort, I managed to pull the nearly drowned Blanca out of the undertow and back to shore. She had forgotten that she could not swim! In my dash to save our beloved Blanca, I lost my eyeglasses in the water. I was unable to read for the remainder of our vacation...

Also that same year, Manolo Gullon, who I mentioned in the beginning of these memoirs, arrived from Spain to live in our home. The end of that same year Blanca got married with a boyfriend that she had met in New York. Since she was not fluent in English and the parish priest was equally not fluent in Spanish, I was inducted as an interpreter to recite their marriage vows. Blanca wore a beautiful white dress, and cut her wedding cake at a reception that we gave her at our home. Blanca had been very good to us. None of the maids that we later "imported" could compare to her caliber. That night, as she was leaving for her honeymoon, our youngest daughter Anna, who was two years old, began to cry...

In New York, I continued to be very active in my civic activities. I continued as President of the Colombian-American Chamber of Commerce. Around that time, the Chancellor German Zea arrived from Colombia in order to attend the Annual Assembly of the United Nations. I was invited to a ceremony in my honor, which took place in the residence of the Consulate General. Chancellor Zea made a small speech and then presented me with the medal of the "Order of San Carlos", for services performed for the Republic of Colombia. With great emotion, I humbly and respectfully responded with a few words of appreciation for being granted such an honor.

It seemed as though we had exerted some influence on some of our important friends, since already three of them had moved with their families, into our neighborhood. We would all get together quite often. They were Pedro Olarte along with his wife Maruja, and Jose Morales and his wife Elena. Pedro and Jose were both members of the Colombian Diplomatic Corp. There was also Hernado Zuleta and his wife Ana Maria. Hernando represented "Paz Del Rio," an important state owned steel company. All our children were friends with theirs. They all attended the same schools. It was quite clear that our children, who were the most numerous, were the leaders of the "gang." They would do the most unlikely pranks. One Halloween Eve, along with Pedro Pablo and Bernardo Olarte, who were a little older, and not content with carrying out the usual mischief such as switching street signs or car license plates; they put together and clothed an adult-sized, very lifelike dummy. They then laid this dummy down in the middle of a main street. An older woman returning home in her car became the victim of this elaborate prank. She slammed on her brakes but was not able to avoid running over this "man" who was sprawled out on the street. This poor woman suffered a heart attack. The police that came to her aid began searching for the culprits of this practical joke that became a near tragedy.

In the city of Larchmont, we had a Sheriff and seven deputies, whom we paid ourselves. They were all such good people, which at times would offer a ride to our children who were returning home late at night, or caught in a rainstorm. It was very easy for them to identify those responsible for this mischief. The Police arrived at our home, with the dummy, and reprimanded the guilty ones.

There were other incidents in which the police intervened. Lucía, who had involved herself in community affairs, was named Girl Scout Troop Leader. Almost all of the girls in her troop attended the same school. On some weekends, they would organize "slumber parties." One evening they arrived at The Girl Scout House with their sleeping bags. After dinner, the girls entertained themselves, and Lucía chaperoned their activities. The girls had stayed up until the early morning hours. Their young boyfriends had congregated outside The Girl Scout House looking for their attention. The girls were so thrilled by all this activity, that they posed themselves near windows in order to get a look at their fan club. Wanting some peace and quiet, Lucía called the police, who immediately cleared the area, and all were able to finally get some sleep.

On another occasion, it was our daughter Joyce's birthday and her friends gave her a surprise party in our home. From very early in the evening, our house was invaded by young people. There were so many of them, that their cars and motorcycles had completely blocked the street. They were everywhere! Lucía and I thought it very unusual that this many people had attended. We called the police, who then asked Joyce if she knew or had invited all these people. Joyce's negative response initiated a mass exodus of these "party crashers," under the watchful eye of the Chief of Police...

With Tom Watson in charge and Vin Learson in command of his legion of distinguished sales people, IBM was flooding the market with its improved System 360. The company was transforming itself into a giant. The price of its shares in the New York Stock Exchange was growing at a tremendous pace. Our production plants could not keep up with the demand. In Japan, IBM inaugurated a new plant in Fujisawa, located near Tokyo, for the production of models 20 and 40 of the System 360... The transmission of data between our plant in San Jose, California and Paris via the COMSAT satellite was tested. Our computer company continued to be the worlds largest. This did not dismay our competitors ---In Japan, General Electric associated itself with Tokyo Shibaura and Mitsubishi Electric in order to produce more computers---Hawker Siddeley Dynamics of England entered the computer market with the DCC-2---General Electric also formalized a patent agreement with AEG-Telefunken in order to produce GE computers for industrial applications, in Germany---Borroughs introduced the 8500 which according to them, was the world's largest computer---ICT introduced three new terminals for its computers, the 7011, 7012 and the 7013---In Windsor, English Electric Computers opened a new plant, thereby doubling its manufacturing capacity---Philips, in an alliance with Siemag, produced their first computer, the EL-2500---In France, General Electric took financial control of Bull---ITT of France in conjunction with the Central Laboratory of Communications produced the small DC-2 and the 825P computers---Siemens announced its new third generation, series 300 computers---Honeywell introduced its 1250 and 125 computers, thereby increasing its 200 series to eight different systems---RCA introduced its new time shared Spectra 70-46 computer---Borroughs came out with the E-4000 series.

In the summer of 1967, in the city of Montreal, the World's Fair by name of "Expo-67," was inaugurated. Since Lucía had attended a school in Montreal and had friends there, we were able to rent an apartment in Montreal with their help. We spent our vacation in this beautiful city. We left our home in Larchmont very early in the morning in our station wagon. We arrived in Montreal the following night. For Lucía it was a joy to be able to see the Boysee Family again. They lived in the nearby city of Saint Lambert, and had been Lucía's hosts there while she had been a student before we were married. The exposition was situated on a small island on the Saint Lawrence River. It was magnificent, with all types of exhibits and diversions that the children enjoyed immensely. We would have breakfast early and then go to the fair. We would return to our apartment at night after visiting and enjoying the many things that Canada had to offer. We returned home via the north east coast of the United States.

Our office in New York continued to grow. Marcial was able to increase the number of personnel, in order to keep up with the large quantity of visitors that were arriving from all over the world. The personnel that he would bring from our European and Asian divisions were very special. They were young, with sales experience and besides being fluent in English, also spoke their native language. For them, it was a great opportunity to spend a few years with us in the United States and then return to their respective countries with invaluable experience that could only help their careers. One extraordinary case was that of Jacques Maisonrouge, who after working in various capacities in IBM of France, was designated Vice-President of IBM World Trade. He ultimately arrived at our office in New York as President of the Company.

The summer of 1968, we spent our summer vacation in the beaches of North Carolina. My old friend Arnold Schiffman had been generous enough to offer me a house that he owned there. Arnold was the President of the American Association of Jewelers. I met him in Colombia in 1947 when he was there buying emeralds from the "Banco de La Republica." He owned a jewelry store in Greensboro, North Carolina and was member of the Rotary Club of that same city. I was a member of the Board of Director's of the Rotary Club of Bogotá. The club had assigned me to assist Mr. Schiffman, since he knew very little Spanish. I picked him up at the airport in Bogotá and accompanied him everywhere during a week. He returned to the United States with a fistful of Colombian emeralds. The "Banco de La Republica" had issued him a receipt for the emeralds, which upon his return was only charged five percent of the customs' duties. Arnold was so grateful, that on one of my trips he put me up in his luxurious Greensboro residence, where I spent a few days before travelling back to New York together.

That vacation in the summer of 1968 was a memorable one. We accepted Arnold's invitation and parted for the shores of North Carolina in our ten-passenger station wagon. We had a luggage rack filled with suitcases. We traveled down the central coast of the United States. It took us two days to arrive to those beautiful beaches. Arnold had lent us a large beach house, and to our children's delight, we discovered three small boats that had been left at our disposal. One day, our son Pierre and Arnold's grandson ventured out in a small sailboat. It was getting late and they were no where to be found, so we alerted the Coast Guard who mounted a search and rescue. That evening, to our relief, the two boys were towed in to our beach in their small boat...

Of all the side excursions that we took during that summer, the one I remember the most was our visit to the sand dunes of Kitty Hawk, North Carolina, where the brothers Orville and Wilbur Wright made aviation history with the first airplane flight. Their small plane flew one hundred meters and landed on the beach. We all had a great time tumbling down on the warm sand of these dunes, where this historical flight had occurred. On our return trip we spent a few days in the nation's capital so that our children could become acquainted with this beautiful and historical city. We brought along with us Gloria Elena, Liliana and Milena Restrepo, who at this moment were there with their father, and they spent a few days with us at our home.

Since we were members of the largest computer company in the world, we had to accept our responsibilities as a corporate citizen in the communities where we lived, and also in the country and in the business world. To the extent that our creed was to compete vigorously, while respecting our competitors and the laws that governed us. Furthermore, we had the obligation to help the surrounding society and demonstrate that we were part of a great company that was trying to better the world with it's technology.

Few things had changed at IBM since the death of our founder. Perhaps the most notable was the color of our machines. In addition, we no longer used starched collars and in our visits to the laboratory, we could see our scientists working in shirt sleeves and without ties. We no longer chanted slogans in our sales training schools, but the basic principles of human relations remained intact. The managers had the obligation to listen to and respect the dignity of the employees working under them. In my entire life with IBM I was never a "yes man", I did not like to adulate my superiors. Many times I disagreed with my superiors and I would demonstrate it if I believed that my proposal would benefit our company. I knew Latin America like the palm of my hand, especially the temperament and character of it's people. That is why sometimes I had to challenge Dick Watson.

One afternoon our new president, Mr. Maisonrouge, called all the general managers to conference. These conferences were made periodically, and after the boss made announcements and reported on the progress of the company, all those present spoke giving their ideas and suggestions. We were around fifty people, and unfortunately, Maisonrouge, with much conceit went on with his speech repeating something that had happened ten years before, without giving specific names, when he had come from France to do a favor for America...

Our new President was referring to my first encounter with him ten years before, that I described many pages back. I was the minuscule person in the story that hadn't recognized him, the modern La Fayette. He wanted to demonstrate how poorly organized our office was before his arrival. I had heard many business speeches before in my life; they almost always included a joke or a funny story to put the audience at ease, but never to denigrate someone. With my eyes closed, in a few seconds my entire pleasing life with the IBM family crossed my mind, where my best friends were my subordinates. I felt something unexplainable! My pulse throbbed in my head and I felt stunned.

When our new President finished his boring speech, I asked to speak and I stood up and said "that indignant person of whom the speaker referred to was me ten years ago. Mr. Maisonrouge, would you please stop mentioning this episode in public, because it doesn't do any good to you, nor to me, nor to IBM." When the meeting was over I went to my office without saying a word to anyone. A few minutes later, he called me and asked me to go to his office. He told me he never thought I would be offended in such a manner. Like a man of character, I responded that I did not regret what I had said...

A short time later I was notified that IBM needed me very far from there... Within the United States but more than 2,000 miles away. I was moved (exiled) to the City of San Francisco, which was our only company office outside of New York. I would initiate and head the office as "Manager of Special Activities". The reason was that important visitors from Asia, mostly from Japan, kept increasing and the City of San Francisco was the port of entry.

When I arrived at home that evening I gathered my family together, as I did with Lucía before our wedding, and I asked them: "If we were to go and live in California which city would you prefer?". Everyone responded at once "San Francisco!". Now I had the approval of my family, which was most important. Of course I could have refused and not accepted the "promotion" and I wouldn't be fired, since that is not customary in IBM, especially now after my incident with the President...

The next day when I returned to my office and I told my colleague friends about my next "exile", they all congratulated me because I would be getting out of the New York "rat race" and that I could be my own boss. As we always did our household moves, I went alone to explore the place where I would work, and figure out where our future home would be, with good schools to continue the education of our seven children. It was a propitious time, now that the summer of 1969 was approaching, the school year was ending and the kids were starting their three-month vacation. I was already familiar with the beautiful city of San Francisco, the most cosmopolitan of all the cities in North America. IBM Domestic already ran a large operation there in three large buildings. I chose the best one in the financial district of the city at 44 Montgomery Street. Then I began to investigate where I would buy my new house. I thought the best region would be south, between the cities of San Francisco and San Jose, where IBM had for many years a large factory, which I would have to visit frequently. Besides, the area was beautiful with good schools and universities.

145

When I returned we began to prepare for our move. We put our beautiful home for sale. I didn't worry if it didn't sell while we were still there; we could leave it to IBM. That plan was part of our benefits. When the company would move us, it was desirable that not only our bodies but our minds be acclimated to our new home without worries. Generally, the major investment that people make is the home where they live. By means of our plan, the property was appraised by both the company and someone chosen by the employee. That is how we arrived at a fair price; the company would then take charge of the property and loan the employee the equivalent for their new investment. In the meantime, if the property sold for less, IBM would lose the difference, but if it sold for more, IBM would send the difference to the employee, and the company would cover the cost of the sales commission.

Our work was so global that we were all used to moving. Jokingly we would use the acronym "I've Been Moved" for IBM. Not only would I have to take care of all my obligations at the office, but also remove my personal belongings. Among my personal wall hangings in my office were three very valuable works of art that belonged to the great collection of IBM. I was given permission to take these on loan to adorn the walls of my new office in San Francisco. Relating to my civic duty, I sent various letters of resignation to the different organizations that I belonged, and to some I called together meetings to designate my successors.

At home everyone seemed content. In June all our children successfully finished their schoolwork and all graduated to the next school year. Joyce our eldest daughter, graduated from High School and was ready to begin University. We turned in our membership at "Orienta Beach Club" our social and sport club, where we spent many wonderful happy moments with our friends the Olartes and the Zuletas. They had left New York just a few months before, so our departure was not so painful. Every move IBM made cost them a fortune, and as customary, we could hire the best experts for our move. They arrived many days in advance packing everything very carefully in special boxes and taking them to a nearby storage. Even though they were trustworthy, everything was insured. The last things they took were the beds.

As was customary in our company, we didn't leave immediately to our destination and we stayed in a hotel of our choice for a few days. That gave us time to take care of last minute details, shopping and to say farewell to Broadway and it's shows. We finally left on a fine morning on a plane that took us to our destination on a non-stop five-hour flight. To accomplish this, the entire family stayed in three rooms at the Hotel Roosevelt in the center of Manhattan. I walked to my office, while my family enjoyed and said farewell to the capital of the world...

CHAPTER EIGHT

IN SAN FRANCISCO

Since we didn't have a home in California, our furnishings, belongings and automobile were in storage until we notified them. In the meantime, we lived with the clothing we had in our numerous suitcases that we brought. We had reservations at the Palo Alto Holiday Inn, which had a good pool and was in the area we definitely wanted to establish our residence. The only thing we removed from storage was our station wagon that arrived intact along with the rest of our belongings.

I started to organize my office in San Francisco, and in the meantime, we dedicated ourselves to finding our future home through many real estate companies. I continued belonging to the Rotary Club, and in that famous world fraternity of men, I met George Lauhban, who was the owner of a real estate company.

We went through an extensive zone of various residential areas from south of San Francisco to the near-by towns where we were staying. One of the houses shown to us was one where Shirley Temple, the famous movie actress, had previously lived.

In order to leave the car for Lucía and the children, I would catch the train at the Palo Alto station that was very close to our Hotel. It was approximately a 40-mile trip and I would arrive in San Francisco in an hour, while I read the morning paper. It was more or less the same thing I did in

New York for many years. The atmosphere one breathed on my floor was much more informal than the one I previously worked in. The people in California were very friendly and open. The manager of that IBM Domestic office was a great collaborator. He gave me a good secretary, whose name was Karen Olsen. Even though she was already familiar with our organization, I put her up to date with the small differences that existed in World Trade, now that she began to work for the entire world.

When the personnel of my floor became aware that "IBM World Trade " had invaded their office, they seemed surprised. My office was different from that of other managers. It was the only one adorned with works of art that belonged to the great collection of IBM. When I arrived to my office and greeted them amiably in the corridors, I intuited that almost all of them felt admiration and respect for me. The surprise was even greater when they saw me departing with one of my guests in a luxurious limousine, and dining with them in the best restaurants of the city...

In my new destination where all my colleagues worked for IBM Domestic, the trauma of another monopoly lawsuit was felt by all, when at the beginning of 1970 the government took legal action against our company. This time we were accused of crushing our competitors - some of them had already taken legal action against us for various motives. The most important one was that of "Control Data", that cost IBM many millions and finally we had to concede and hand over our "service bureau" division. For all these reasons "Uncle Sam" wanted to break IBM apart into many pieces, as they had done with many other corporations in the past. Our investors panicked and our stock went down to half of its previous value. The lawsuit lasted almost thirteen years, during which our competitors grew considerably. For this reason and due to the lack of resources to continue battling against IBM, the government abandoned their lawsuit during the Presidency of Ronald Reagan.

The majority of my visitors were Mexican and Japanese executives. Since I did not speak Japanese I asked IBM of Japan for an assistant. They sent me the best one they had to carry out this job. His name was Yoshiki Suga, a young man who had been educated in Japanese and North American Universities. I got him an office next to mine, and I noticed how pleased he was for the promotion he had obtained. His job was to take care of only our customers that arrived from Japan, and I took care of the rest of the world. I suggested that if his customers were very important, that he bring them to my office to introduce them to me. I enjoyed watching "Yoshi" display his culture, when he would bow deeply to the Presidents of large Japanese Corporations.

After a lot of searching, we found the house that suited us. It was on top of a hill on an acre of land, surrounded by apricot orchards in Los Altos Hills. Our address was 12143 Hilltop Drive, and we needed to do some work on it as it had not been completely finished. An oddity was that our home included a small stable; it was not unusual for homes in this rural setting to have a stable for horses, where horseback riding was common and people kept their horses on their property. It was mandatory in this township to own at least one acre of land, which made it a very pleasant area to live in.

We closed on our house and the moving company installed all of our belongings in our new residence. We went to live there immediately. The first thing we did was to enroll our children in school, which would start very

151

soon, after three months of vacation. The older ones would continue at Los Altos High School, my son Pierre would attend Covington Junior High School and the two youngest at Eastbrook Elementary School. Our oldest daughter Joyce wanted to travel to Colombia, and went to live there for a time with her Grandmother.

We purchased another car for me and Lucía continued driving the station wagon. I would rarely drive the 40-mile trip to my office in San Francisco. Even though the magnificent new 280 freeway was near our home, I preferred driving just a few miles to the train station in Palo Alto where I could park my car all day until my return. Many times it was quite comfortable for me, when my work consisted of demonstrating the System 7 in Palo Alto, or if the entire day was spent in San Jose. I could drive there in half an hour to the south, where five thousand people worked for IBM. Today that region is called Silicon Valley where all of our modern competitors are. We were the first to arrive there with our factory, where the "Ramac" system was first invented and manufactured, later with our laboratory in Los Gatos.

Our San Jose factory was made famous in 1959 when Tom Watson along with the U.S. Government chose it for the Russian ruler Nikita Khrushchev to tour in order to see U.S. industry. The visit commenced with dining in the cafeteria together with Tom Watson, tray in hand, with all the workers of the factory. Since he brought with him a very good interpreter he asked questions of our workers about what they were earning, if they were happy, or what were their major problems at work. It is said that when he asked that to one of our workers, they answered "my major problem is in the morning, looking for a parking space". The visit ended with a demonstration of the "Ramac" System, when our illustrious visitor asked what had occurred in our world year by year since Adam and Eve until now...

The first thing we did to our home was to finish an upstairs bedroom and bath, and to install a swimming pool so that the entire family could swim there that very summer. I had never witnessed in my life such a fast and efficient job. We contracted a pool specialist that installed it from start to finish in one week! It all started with a back hoe that excavated it the first day, then gunite cement, plumbing, plaster, tiles, filter and heater, diving board and slide so that in just one week the children were plunging and diving in.

Autumn arrived and our children started school. An efficient school bus system picked the children up in the morning, they had lunch at school, and brought them home in the afternoon. They all liked the more liberal system here. The only mandatory subjects were math, English, science and physical education. They had a variety of electives such as foreign languages, art, etc., and they could make their own choices.

The seasons of the year were two: the yellow and the green. The winter was green and it rained often. The summer was yellow and it wouldn't rain for six months. The climate was moderate where we lived, it was never too cold. But in San Francisco, the entire year seemed the same; somewhat cold because of the summer fog. I would return home from my office dressed warmly, to don my bathing suit, and while we swam I would fire up the barbecue next to the pool, and then we would dine in the fresh air.

I continued as a member of The Rotary Club of San Francisco which, like the one in New York, was the largest that I had known. We would meet weekly for lunch in a large hotel in front of my office. Since we were so many we couldn't get to know everyone. I always preferred the smaller clubs where it was easier to fraternize. It served me well in life especially in countries where we were just starting out. I immediately met the best lawyer who would create our by-laws, and our future customers. I remember that when I worked with Dick Watson, I convinced him to join our club and I took it upon myself to introduce him and he was accepted into the New York club. In the beginning he attended some meetings. However, the by-laws of the Rotary Club indicate that if someone misses three consecutive meetings without just cause, he is out of the club. Since Dick was such a busy man and spent the major part of his life traveling, he had to abandon his membership. In San Francisco many visiting customers arrived who were Rotarians, who I could assist with their businesses through the members in our club.

1970 arrived, which was a fateful year for IBM. In March Dick Watson resigned from his job with our company and accepted the post as the U.S. Ambassador in France. It was a great honor for Dick and his family, but we all knew that he departed from IBM sadly and with some resentment, because of his failure when his brother put him in charge of production of the System 360. Even though I had many discussions with Dick, when we disagreed on related matters as to how we should handle our business in Latin America, I was saddened by his departure. After all, we both wanted the same end, the best for IBM, for our customers and our employees, who I knew so well because I had been born and raised in it's culture. We also knew each other very well because I reported directly to Dick when I returned from my extensive trips to the countries south of the Rio Grande, and he would approve my decisions...

It seemed that the Watson dynasty was going to extinguish when in that same year Tom Watson suffered a heart attack, at the early age of 57. Inside and outside of IBM there was great commotion, because the outcome still wasn't known. Even though the company was in good hands with Vin Learson in charge, Wall Street was shaken up and shares went down 50% that year. Tom recuperated and two months later returned to the office to present his resignation. The Board of Directors did not accept it and asked him to continue reducing his workload. IBM headquarters relocated to a beautiful building surrounded by trees and lawns in the Armonk area, near Tom's home, and much to his regret, he continued going to the office. He was a multimillionaire, whose doctors told him that he had to take very good care of himself. Besides, he had things on his mind that he wanted to do when he retired from business. His two passions were aviation and navigation. His yacht "Palawan" was waiting for him...

June 29, 1971 was a very emotional day, when in every IBM office in the world Tom Watson's speech pronouncing his resignation from his post in IBM was heard. He had headed the company for 15 years of the 35 years that he had worked for IBM. He was designated a member of the executive committee until his retirement, which in those days was at 60 years of age. That day the Watson dynasty was over, which at first was seen as nepotism. Vin Learson took his place, who only had a year and a half left before retirement. Frank Cary was the executive who was being groomed to run IBM. Frank began his career in California in the 1950's. He did outstanding work in every post he had, and he was ready for this leadership role.

Richard Nixon was the president of the United States, and the whole country was in turmoil. The cause was the war in Vietnam. All the younger generation was against that armed intervention. The universities and schools were transformed into centers of protest. Since there was mandatory military service, many young men at the age of 18 were mobilized into this unjust war. On a certain occasion, President Nixon visited the city of San Jose near our home. My older children confessed to me that they took part in a demonstration there in which rocks were thrown at the President.

Our daughter Karen, who liked animals very much, acquired a lovely puppy and named it "zephyr". The dog kept growing and would swim in the pool with our children. Since dogs ran loose, it was the law to license and put name tags on their collars. Zephyr became a wanderer and got caught many times by the dogcatcher and taken to the pound. Poor Karen would spend her weekly allowance that we gave her to get her dog back. Many times the dog would arrive in a luxurious automobile whose owner had found him lost very far from home. One day Karen decided to give Zephyr a birthday party and invited all the dogs in the neighborhood with their owners. All the guests arrived very tame, and the party went along fine while they tasted some treats. Suddenly an unhappy guest started a fight that transformed into a real pitched battle between all those present and between one bite and another, the party was over...

Henry Rasmussen, a good friend and businessman called me from Colombia. He said he wanted to marry my sister-in-law Alicia, Lucía's sister, and asked me to make the necessary arrangements for a civil ceremony at San Francisco City Hall. They arrived together from Bogotá, they married and spent some time with us in our home. Also from Colombia, Milena Restrepo arrived who spent six months with us and went to High School with our children.

Next to our property was an acre lot that was put on the market for sale. It was on top of our hill, and had an excellent view in all four directions. We bought it and became owners of our small hill, which we called "Rancho Grande" in memory of our last residence in Colombia.

We hired a good architect to draw up some plans for a Spanish California ranch-style house, one level with no stairs, and adequately comfortable for our family. We showed the plans to our friend Dean Miller, a young contractor. The idea was to build the ideal home for us and to sell the other one. Dean began to build it. He and his workers would do the labor and we would purchase the materials. Everything was very special, we even had the hand-made red tiles for the roof brought from Mexico.

In June Karen and Luis graduated from Los Altos High School. Our children looked so fine receiving their diplomas, dressed in the traditional cap and gown. Afterwards we had a great celebration in our home, now that this was the first time that a daughter and son graduated at the same time. Continuing the celebration we all went together on vacation touring and getting to know the great state of California. Things that remain in my memory are the impressive natural beauty of Yosemite National Park, Sequoia National Park, or the man-made beauty of the William Randolf Hearst Castle...

Since I was no longer at the general headquarters of the company, where we got first-hand knowledge of our activities and that of our competitors in the entire world, my first hand information came from Japan, now that San Francisco was its port of entry. The "Japanese Miracle" whose industry had invaded the United States with its automobiles, televisions and all its electronic industry, was also first in line with computers. In Japan 48% of the computers were made in Japan, 40% were IBM, and the other 12% were Univac together with the foreign companies that associated with the Japanese companies, in order to get into their gigantic market.

My friend Marcial Digat also retired, and I no longer had fellow friends from the olden times. Also our company was continuing to get more impersonal. That was the result of its great size and the enormous amount of new people that increased our ranks. Young individuals, real geniuses in new techniques in modern electronics were recruited and we had to make way for them so that IBM wouldn't stagnate and stand up to the competition that every day was more aggressive. In the meantime, the "old guard" was forming a bureaucracy that was no longer necessary. Speaking sincerely, I also belonged to that bureaucracy and retired when I completed 38 years of continuous service...

The day of my retirement, when I returned home, my children had organized a party for me. They had covered the walls with posters representing the metamorphosis of my persona. In some showing the day I arrived, dressed as an elegant businessman with a tie and briefcase. The others depicting me converted into a "hippie" with a beard and long hair. I believe they were fortune-telling prophets, because from that moment on I have never again shaved my beard...

The executives from our principal office in New York invited me to a farewell banquet. Together with Lucía, we traveled in a luxurious airplane with a bar and piano on board. The flight took five hours and Lucía showed her talent on the piano. The luncheon was celebrated in the conference room of IBM World Trade, located at 821 United Nations Plaza. After the speeches, in which my personality, my loyalty and my perseverance were exalted, they gave Lucía and me some valuable gifts. I answered very emotionally, and I never again entered that building, from which I had removed myself three years before...

When I started my life with IBM in the year 1933, we were a small family spread out around the world. Now we were many thousands of people who did not recognize each other, that for me were just names written in the books of office personnel. But in the Spanish speaking world, to which I had dedicated most of my life, the family remained in my mind and in my heart. Many had ascended and were directing the destiny of the company. I knew them all personally and they were part of my IBM family. Now that IBM was so big, and it was almost impossible to name them all, I render tribute to those that managed Spain, the Mother Country, and Latin America the day of my retirement. The following are their names:

Spain	Fernando de Asua	President
Argentina	Benito Esmerode	General Manager
Bahamas and Bermuda	E. H. White	General Manager
Barbados and Grenada	U. M. Asiu	General Manager
Bolivia	E. Badani	General Manager
Brazil	J. B. A. Amorim	President
Chile	H. Elizalde	General Manager
Colombia	Enrique Rugeles	General Manager
Costa Rica	Marco Aurelio Soto	General Manager
Dominican Republic	H. Thommen	General Manager

Ecuador	R. Gracia Lago	General Manager
El Salvador	G. Osorio	General Manager
Guatemala	M. Marroquin	General Manager
Honduras	J. M. Covelo	General Manager
Mexico	J. A. Guerra	President
Nicaragua	E. Ojeda	General Manager
Panama	Rogelio Alfaro	President
Paraguay	U. S. Varela	Manager
Peru	Miguel Checa	President
Uruguay	A. M. Aizpun	General Manager
Venezuela	S. Covelo	President

CHAPTER NINE

APPENDIX

After our farewell trip to New York, we returned to our home in California. Surely I was going to miss my work at IBM. Half the active life of any normal person is their work. When I married and had a family, I became accustomed to not bringing my preoccupations at work to my home. I also would draw a line to not take my worries from home to my work. Some of my friends died one year after their retirement. Their work was the most important thing in their life, and for them an empty space impossible to fill remained. For that reason, IBM founded a department that worked to send us newsletters prior to and in anticipation of our retirement, to advise us to begin acquiring new hobbies and projects and to develop our talents and new interests that would replace our work. I had already elaborated my agenda for the future.

The first thing I did was to return to the university, and give myself the pleasure to mingle with young people. I not only saw how education had changed over the years, but I was also going to learn some things that would serve me in the future. I enrolled in two classes at Foothill College, where my daughter Karen studied art. Since I loved plants I began to study botany, and also modern sculpture, where I learned to use new materials and basic principles that were not known before.

To plant a tree one needed special techniques in order

for it to grow healthy and rapidly. My first project was to plant twenty Italian cypresses that would divide our property from the one next door where we were building the house. I ordered some very special trees from Los Angeles and planted them in some well-fertilized soil. Many years later, I returned to California and passed near to what once had been my home, ecstatically viewing my twenty large cypresses growing so lushly...

In May of 1972 our daughter Anna, the youngest, received her first Holy Communion. One month later in the same church in Los Altos was Michele's Confirmation. A few days later Michele gave us one of the greatest joys that a daughter could give. We all attended her graduation from Covington Junior High, when her name was called, and no surprise to us, the principal made special mention saying that Michele was not only top in her class but also had the highest score for the whole school that year. At this same time Denise graduated from Los Altos High School and curiously one of her electives was auto mechanics...

Candelaria, Lucía's mother, came to spend a few months with us. Everyone speaks terribly about their mother-in-laws, but in that respect, I am the luckiest man in the world. I never had even the slightest problem or argument with her. She was very discrete, and very successfully transmitted her great qualities to the woman who I married. I remember I would take walks with her in the late afternoon in the fruit orchards that surrounded our property. We would pick the sweetest and ripest apricots and would eat them until we could eat no more...

The house we were building was almost finished and it looked fantastic from all angles. We were in the middle of summer and we had all finished all of our classes. Without anything set on the agenda, each one of us did as we pleased. Lucía would watch us all and she would see that I would take off my pajamas in the mornings, would put on my swim suit, and in the evening, would take off my swim suit and put my pajamas on again. Aside from taking care of my plants, swimming a few times during the day, and lighting the grill by the pool for the evening's barbecue, I wasn't doing much else. Lucía, who thought I was getting bored, after seeing me so active all of my life, one day said: "why don't we leave all of this and return to Colombia?" And I responded: "and what can I do in Colombia at this point in my life?" Lucía immediately responded, leaving me without words: "what is it that you cannot do in Colombia?"...

The decision was made quickly, even though this time we wouldn't be making the move with IBM, who not only took care of everything, but paid the tab too. We sold our houses and our cars. We got rid of a lot of unnecessary things and we hired a moving company that would pack everything in light-weight containers since we would send everything by air from San Francisco to Bogotá. We stayed a few days in a hotel in Palo Alto and said good-bye to our friends and in August 1972, we departed from San Francisco airport. Our flight made a stop in Miami and the whole family arrived in Bogotá - all 10 of us - including the Grandmother of my children...

We stayed at the Military Club, which worked out well for us since it had an olympic size pool and sports facilities. We did the most urgent things - we registered Pierre in the Colegio Nueva Granada and Michele and Anna in the Colegio de las Hermanas Benedictinas (St. Benedict's Academy). We bought a car and started house hunting. We found one and rented it - an old mansion on Calle 76 - one block away from the Gimnasio Moderno.

Many years ago I had bought a parcel of land in Bogotá and a small beach plot on the Caribbean Sea; I had not paid much attention to these properties except for paying the yearly taxes due. The lot in Bogotá was two hectares and was north of the city, in what today is called the area of "Cedritos". I hired a contractor who came up with blueprints to construct a subdivision of 40 houses. Since I didn't know much about construction, I named as supervisor of the construction a young architect, Hernando Groot. The subdivision was named "Rancho Grande" in memory of the house we used to live in.

The houses sold like hot cakes at a half a million pesos each and now they are selling for a little over a hundred million pesos each! Hernando and his brother Alberto, who is an engineer, founded a building and construction company by the name of "Futuro", and finished many different construction projects in north Bogotá. I also founded my own company "Inversiones Rancho Grande" and named Hernando as General Manager and I serve as President. We both have made money with this endeavor, and even though the company is in recess now, Hernando has always managed my interests with the utmost honesty when I have been traveling out of the country for long periods of time.

As far as the plot of land on the Caribbean Sea, the whole family went to go check it out, thinking that it would possibly become a place for our vacation home. The beach was called "El Frances" and it was just north of the town of Tolu. When I originally bought this land many years ago, it was covered with palm trees. I was greatly disappointed when we saw it after so many years, to find that all the palm trees were gone. That, and the fact that it had been invaded by the neighbors, forced me to sell the property.

In January 1973, I did something I had always dreamt of doing. I knew the entire American continent, but I always traveled by air, visiting on business the capitals and the main cities of each and every country, but never going into the interior of each country. With my friend, Enrique Saenz, we traveled through the countryside from Bogotá to the Patagonia, the southern tip of the continent, in a Renault 4. I would drive in the mornings and Enrique would drive in the afternoons. We drove 25,000 kilometers (15,500 miles) roundtrip in two months. The roads were very poor but very picturesque. We would stay more time in the places we liked. When we were in Cuzco, Peru, we took a train to Machu Pichu. In Bolivia, from Lake Titicaca we drove to La Paz. We entered Argentina through the Province of Salta. This border crossing was very interesting. The Bolivian soldier that waved good-bye to us was barefoot and with a tattered uniform. Half a mile up the road, in the Argentine border patrol station, our passports were stamped by some soldiers who wore impeccable German-style uniforms and boots. We crossed the whole province of Salta and then Tucuman and Rosario. Finally we arrived in Buenos Aires, were we stayed a few days and where we saw the Formula One car race.

Enrique filmed the whole trip on his 16 millimeter camera and later added music and titles. Since it was summer time in Argentina, we also stayed at Mar del Plata. From Bahia Blanca we crossed over to Bariloche. From Llao-Llao we crossed the Andes Mountains to the southern part of Chile. We arrived in Santiago where we stayed a few days in the Hotel Carrera. This was when President Allende was in power. The country was going through harsh economic times. The money was so devaluated that we would get many thousands of Chilean Pesos for one U.S. Dollar. The hotel room cost the equivalent of two dollars a night, and it was full of Cuban and Chinese consultants. We bought two cases of very fine Chilean wine. One we drank on the return trip and the other we enjoyed with our families, once back in Colombia.

From Santiago, Chile, to Lima, Peru, the highway was very good - a very well kept section of the Panamerican Highway. But after Peru, it worsened all through Ecuador and Colombia. We returned to Bogotá after being on the road for two months, and most incredibly, with the same car! We only had to change one tire. The executives of Renault, when they heard of our feat, asked Enrique to sell them the movie, where you could see the car crossing rivers, climbing the snow peaked Andes, etc...

When we arrived in Bogotá from San Francisco, our daughter Joyce was already famous. She was a candidate for the Ms. Bogotá Beauty Pageant, a theater actress and was now opening her first individual art exhibit in the Ateneo Dianarte Gallery in the city of Cali. She and her sister Karen had shown great abilities and talent since a very young age in the art of drawing and painting.

In May of 1973 we went on vacation to the Islands of San Andres and Providencia. Later in June, Michele's best friend, Karla Albright, came to visit from Los Altos and with Anna, the four of us went to Santa Marta on the "Expreso del Sol" a passenger train that no longer exists, which arrived six hours late. Pierre excelled in sports at the Colegio Nueva Granada, especially in wrestling. Many times we would go see him compete at the El Salitre stadium.

Enrique Rugeles, who was the General Manager of

IBM in Colombia, proposed that I talk to the executives of the company and tell them of my experiences and the latest sales techniques in the U.S. I accepted with pleasure and gave several conferences and I was later invited by Enrique to many important meetings of the company, especially the "Quarter Century Club" meetings. I was also invited to participate in something that was very sad for me. It was a mass at the Church of San Diego, in memory of Dick Watson, who had unexpectedly passed away in an accident in the U.S. It was 1974 at the time, and he had already resigned from his post as U.S. Ambassador to France. He was the boss that I had reported to directly for the longest period "in my life with IBM", in good times and in bad. We made some small mistakes together, but the majority of the time our decisions were good ones and they were ones that brought success to the company. In our free time, we would enjoy playing golf or poker together during some of our trips through South America...

With my friend Rafael Vargas, we founded a small import and export company, "Refimport". The main objective of the company was to increase trade between Colombia and Russia. We wanted to increase sales of coffee and banana and add products such as textiles, leather goods and fresh-cut flowers. At the same time, we would import watches, telephones and other goods from Russia. Alberto Samper joined the company as a partner. He had been president of Bavaria, a large beer manufacturer in Colombia. With Alberto, we hooked up with the ANDI (National Association of Industrial Development) in Bogotá and Medellin and we were able to obtain the representation of the 40 largest manufacturers in Colombia. We organized a large exposition in Moscow to show what Colombian industry had to offer. We also presented part of the "Gold Museum" from the Banco de la Republica. At this time the leader of the Russian government was Leonidas Brezhnev and the President of Colombia was Julio Cesar Turbay, who has traveling through Europe at the time and who had promised to attend the opening of the expo in Russia. Apparently, Turbay liked Paris more and we had to open the show without him. We traveled to Russia several other times, but our business with the Russians did not prosper because it was very difficult to negotiate with the Soviet government.

Even though we didn't make any money, we had a great time seeing and participating in the marvels of Russia, such as the Kremlin, the Hermitage Museum, the Bolshoi Ballet, etc. We would maintain good relations with the members of the Embassy of Colombia. With them we did several side trips close to Moscow, near the Moscow River. In the same year, with Alberto Samper I crossed that same river swimming and a few months later, I walked over the river covered with three feet of solid ice. Also with Alberto during the summer months we spent a few days on the beaches of the Black Sea. There we took a ship that took us to Yalta and from there, we took a train and crossed the territories of Romania and Bulgaria during two days and two nights. We passed the Dardanelles strait and finished our journey in Turkey. Nowadays, Alberto is very sick and unconscious. When I go to visit him, he doesn't recognize me...

It was dangerous to live in a house in Bogotá since thieves visited us frequently, jumping fences and breaking into our house, so we decided to do what all of our friends were doing. In 1975 a 12-story building was being constructed a block away from the house we were renting. We designed and bought the duplex penthouse apartment. We moved in and have lived there ever since. Among other things, we have five bedrooms, five baths and on the top floor (12th floor), I have my green house where I dedicate many hours of my day to my favorite hobby, the art of "Bonsai". I was elected during two consecutive years President of the Colombian Association of Bonsai and I still am an active member and travel every year to their annual international convention that this year was in Sydney, Australia.

On September 16, 1975 our daughter Karen, revealed herself as a great artistic painter. That day was the opening of an exposition in the Exposur Gallery in the city of Cali. There was a lot of media coverage on her works and that was the start of Karen's great artistic career. She is nowadays recognized internationally, and she even has her own web-page on the internet.

Another revelation was that of our daughter Michele. In June of 1976 she graduated from High School and she continued the tradition that she had started in the U.S. when she received her scholarship back in 1972 since she had the highest grades of her graduating 8th grade class. This time, they gave her an award for having the highest grades in the history of the school. That same year I made an unforgettable trip to Greece and Egypt. It was a tour organized by my friend Andres Holguin, which ended in a splendid cruise through the Aegean Sea.

Both of our sons decided to enlist in the Armed Forces of Uncle Sam. I never opposed their own decisions, they were adult men and U.S. citizens. My oldest son Luis enlisted in the Army and Pierre in the Navy. For them it was an experience and discipline, which they decided to resign from some time later.

At the beginning of 1978, our eldest daughter Joyce got married to Alfonso Villegas. They went on their honeymoon to Europe and I met up with them in Hamburg, Germany, where Karen and four other Colombian artists were opening an art exhibit. This exposition was sponsored by the Colombian Consulate and was later taken to Berlin. The newlyweds continued on to Greece and since I had a Eurail-Pass for two months, I decided to wander through those worlds...

Our first granddaughter Juana, daughter of Joyce, was born on September 26, 1978 and we baptized her on October 10. Her paternal aunt, Emma Villegas de Gaitan, was her Godmother, and I was her Godfather. In December of that same year, our daughter Michele married Hector Buitrago. They met at the University of Los Andes, where Hector obtained his law degree. They had their first daughter, our second granddaughter, Andrea, who was born on August 1, 1979.

When our daughter Anna was fifteen, we gave her as a birthday present a trip to the Far East. Lucía, Anna and I flew from Bogotá to Los Angeles, and continued to Japan, Hong Kong, China, Thailand, Singapore, the Philippines and Hawaii. We returned back to Bogotá through the U.S. It was a long but unforgettable trip.

In January of 1982, my brother-in-law and long-time friend, Henry Rasmussen called me from Florida and told me: "Meet me tomorrow at the Bogotá airport. Get an appointment at Marly Hospital, because my doctor's here tells me that I have a very advanced stage of cancer and that I have ten days to live." I was with him every day and ten days later, he died...

In May of 1982 I went to Leticia, Colombia, a city on

the southern border with Peru, because I wanted to travel on the Amazon River. Navigating on that grand river I had the opportunity to see the indigenous tribes of Peru and Brazil and be close to monkeys and crocodiles...

On June 29 our daughter Anna graduated from high school at Colegio Santa Maria (previously Colegio de las Hermanas Benedictinas). I went to Florida to an apartment that I bought in Palm Beach. While there, I received the fatal news that my brother-in-law, Alvaro, had died in Rome on July 4. Alvaro was on vacations with his wife in Europe and died of a heart attack at the age of 47. His remains were flown to Bogotá and his funeral was the 11th of July in Bogotá.

The whole family enjoyed our apartment in Palm Beach. We did several trips to Florida and I would take advantage of those trips to attend several international Bonsai conventions. In addition, in 1984 I returned to the university. I enrolled in some history courses at the University of Bristol in England, and I also did some side trips to Bath, Stone Henge and Brighton Beach. I ended the trip in London and saw Niky Lauda win a Formula One race.

In Bogotá, I would continue to go to our Monday night poker games that we had started many years ago in the Club Anglo-Americano. I was the oldest member there since some of our friends had returned to their respective countries or had passed away. When that club dissolved, we moved our weekly poker sessions to the Club 74. With Lucía we have also continued playing bridge. Clearly, Lucía plays much better than I do, since she plays almost everyday with her friends and she continues taking some classes. In contrast, I have never taken a bridge class in my life. Nonetheless, as a couple, we continue to win some duplicate bridge games at the Club de Bridge...

In June of 1985 Lucía and I departed on a long journey to the United States and Europe which lasted two years. I left my friend Hernando Groot in charge of my affairs in Colombia. I even left my 57 Thunderbird in one of his country homes. First we visited our children and friends in Florida, Atlanta, California and New York. Then, in Scotland, we enrolled in a course at Stirling University, coinciding with the art festival of Edinburgh. In London we visited the Girault family, except for Joyce and Raymond, who were in France. We flew from London to Biarritz, where Raymond picked us up at the airport and took us to an apartment he had rented for us in Saint Jean de Luz, right on the beach, near theirs.

We saw Joyce, Raymond, and the Feres every day on the beach and at almost every dinner and trip. We had a lot to talk about, considering Raymond and I are the same age, began working for IBM at the same time, in many cases in the same office, and retired at the same time, he in France and I in the States.

In order to ease our travels through Europe we bought a Ford Fiesta. This car behaved very well; it was made in a European factory, and we got the best out of it in every country with our tourist license plates. When we had no engagements, we would drive to Spain in half an hour and have lunch in San Sebastian. Sometimes we would leave early in the morning headed for Biarritz, Lourdes, or to Pau, in the center of the French Pyrenees, where my father was born...

When the North Atlantic began to get cold we moved South with the birds. We entered Spain through Figueras. Salvador Dali was there in the last days of his life. I knew him from when we lived in New York. We went to his famous house to see him but it was not possible, for his butler told us he was in terrible shape that day. We continued on to Barcelona, and then through the Mediterranean coast toward Malaga. There we got in touch with the honorary consul of Colombia, who advised us on where the best place to rent an apartment was. Torremolinos it was, half and hour away from Malaga, in a beautiful building near the beach. We had as much fun as we did in the south of France, though with a better climate.

Every day we visited different parts of AndaLucía and returned to our apartment at night. We went everywhere: Marbella, Puerto Banus, Granada, Cordoba, and Sevilla. In this beautiful city Lucía was robbed of her purse on the street; in it were her documents and our credit cards. We were left without money until new credit cards were sent to us from Madrid. Meanwhile, the scoundrels had a ball buying things with our cards...

Since our luggage increased progressively with everything Lucía bought, we had a trunk made especially to fit in the back of our car. It was made by an expert craftsman from Malaga, and it spent a long time in the trunk of the car, for it was never taken out into any of the hotels we stayed at. We also went to Gibraltar, and from Algeciras we took a boat to Africa. We stayed in Ceuta and its surroundings because we weren't able to obtain a visa to continue to the interior of the continent. Once we were saturated with AndaLucía we proceeded to Madrid, where we were reunited with all of my old friends. At the Oñate home I saw almost all of them, some whom I hadn't seen for the past forty years...

We returned to France through the Riviera. In February of 1986 we stayed in Nice, and saw the famous carnival. Since I never forget IBM, while in Nice I remembered that close by was our famous laboratory of "La Gaude". We drove up the mountains through a picturesque road of the French countryside. At our arrival we were shown the new things our European scientists were creating, we had lunch there, and we returned to Nice that afternoon.

We continued to Montecarlo where we spent a few days gambling in the new casino. Then in Italy: Genova, Portofino, Rome, Villa D'Este. On to the south through Naples, and finally embarked on a ferry to Messina, in the island of Sicily, car and all. We saw the entire island, which is beautiful, with monuments from every century and every culture: Teormina, Cosenza, and Palermo, where a famous mobster trial was going on at the time.

We returned to the continent and continued to the south through the heel of the Italian boot towards Bari, then Milan and Pavia, where we visited my mother's relatives. My first cousin, Lina Protti, 93, was still living. With her were Nadir Grandi, his wife Augusta, and their daughters Alessandra and Elisabetta.

Crossing the Alps, next to the snow covered Mont Blanc, we headed toward Paris, where we spent part of the month of March. We sold the car, which was unnecessary in a city with great public transportation. Besides, we were in a hurry to return to America to meet our new granddaughter Laura, who was born on the twenty seventh of January of 1986. On the twentieth of April she was baptized in Marietta. Margie Taylor was her godmother and I her godfather. My experience as a father of five daughters led me to predict that by her way of crying and smiling, hers will be a happy life with future inclinations for the arts...

That summer we spent traveling between Atlanta and Palm Beach, where we had our apartment. There we were visited by Elvira Samper as well as Ismael Arensburg. In November, Lucía and I took a trip to Mexico. We went to Cancun, Cozumel, and Tulum. In December we returned to Atlanta to spend Christmas with our children and grand-daughters. We traveled in a Honda that turned out to be a very good car, as it withstood the seven hundred miles that separate Florida and Georgia, which we would do in one day.

In February of 1987 we took a boat trip to the Bahamas. We returned to Atlanta to celebrate Andrea's first Holy Communion on the fifth of April, and then with the Buitrago family we went back to Palm Beach for Anna's birthday, on the twenty fourth of April. Pierre came as well and we had a wonderfully "tight" family reunion...

My son-in-law Hector Buitrago deserves an honorable mention. When Hector received his law degree at the Universidad de los Andes, Michele worked for Coca-Cola of Colombia. He was practicing law in Bogotá when Michele was offered a transfer to their company headquarters in Atlanta. Together they moved to the United States to test their luck, as did the fugitive brains of Colombia. While Michele proved her intelligence at Coca-Cola, Hector enrolled at Georgia State University to obtain his degree in law while working at a restaurant. When Laura was born, he would take her to the university, drop her off at the nursery, and he would go to his studies. When his day of classes was done, he would pick her up and go home where they were joined by Andrea, who by that time was dropped off by the school bus. When Michele came back from work Hector would go to his night job at the restaurant. This went on for a long time, until he obtained another degree, this one for the practice of law in the United States, and now he works for Uncle Sam in Atlanta...

After such a long trip, we finally arrived in our home in Colombia on the sixth of May of 1987. In June, Juana left for Atlanta to visit her cousins. I set out to do something I had never done before. At my old age it occurred to me to have my first individual art show. It consisted of several pieces done with paint and collage, representing different days in various Florida locations. I was generously offered the exposition hall of the Chamber of Commerce, and on the thirtieth of September the show opened with a cocktail party to which many friends attended, and lasted until the tenth of October.

In November of 1987 Ismael Arensburg and I set out on a journey to Argentina. We visited the Iguazu Falls, and I was very pleased to be invited to the annual party of IBM of Argentina, where I was reunited with my old friends. In La Plata I saw my friends from my youth, and profound sentiments embraced me as I retraced my childhood steps...

I returned home for Christmas and greeted the New Year, 1988. In February a tremendous explosion occurred which destroyed the windows in our apartment; it was a powerful terrorist bomb that was placed in the headquarters of the Occidental Petroleum Company, very near our apartment. On the twenty sixth of April our daughter Denise married John Ehret in San Francisco. On the thirtieth our granddaughter Juana had her first Holy Communion at the Colegio Nueva Granada. In May Lucía traveled to San Francisco and Atlanta. On the twenty sixth of that month, as president of the Colombian Bonsai Association, I presented the "Oriental Garden" at the Museo del Chico to the mayor of Bogotá, Julio Cesar Sanchez. It was a gift to the city, and I offered it with a speech.

On the twelfth of July I left for San Antonio, Texas, in order to attend the International Bonsai Convention. Then I met up with Pierre in Los Angeles, and together we visited the Bonsai collections in the homes of John Naka and Ben Oki. I continued to San Francisco to meet Anna, Denise, and John. Then to Atlanta: Juana was there and we had great fun with the whole family at the pool and on Hector's boat in Lake Lanier.

I returned to Colombia and on the second of December I was honored with the investiture of Knight of The Order of the Holy Sepulchre of Jerusalem. My friends Ricardo Triana, Ramon Meira, and Antonio Lattanzio already belonged to this order which was established in the Vatican.

Lucía traveled to San Francisco to attend Anna's wedding to John Atkinson on the tenth of December of 1988. A short while later the three traveled back to Colombia where we had a great party for them. On the sixth of March we celebrated my eightieth birthday with many events. Our son Luis was in Bogotá and together with him, Lucía and Elvira Samper I went to the bicycle race course "Primero de Mayo" and went around the race-track on my bicycle a few times while Elvira filmed me. In the afternoon we had a private mass with my intimate friends in a chapel near our home, and at night a great party with musicians but without too much excess.

The twentieth of April Lucía and I parted for the Holy Land on a pilgrimage organized by The Order of the Holy Sepulchre of Jerusalem. There were twenty-five of us and we were accompanied by Monsignors Arturo Franco, Luis Carlos Ferreira, and Manuel Ricaurte. The first stop was Rome, where we met the Pope. We also saw Gonzalo Canal, who was working at the Colombian Embassy. We went to St. Francis of Assisi, and lastly, Prince Pablo Massimo Lanceloti, who has the highest investiture of the Order, held a reception for us in his mansion. Then we flew to Tel - Aviv, "Hill of Spring," and we followed the steps of Jesus: Yaffa, the valley of Samaria, the desert of Judea, Cafarnaun, Mount Carmelo, Mount Tabor and the Mount of Beatitudes. We attended mass every day, and when there was not a church nearby, one of our three prelates presided a field mass. On the Jordan River, in the exact place where John the Baptist performed his baptismal ceremonies, we stopped to contemplate the river, which lies under millenary cypresses. I picked up some seeds that had fallen from the trees, and took them to germinate in Colombia, where today they adorn my bonsai collection.

We went to Nazareth, saw Saint Joseph's carpentry, and then headed toward Jerusalem. The Wailing Wall, the Mount of Olives, the cemetery. In Jerusalem my pilgrim friends gave me the privilege of reading the fourteen Stations of the Cross. Then we had a mass at the Holy Sepulchre by our Monsignors. At the Patriarchate we were received by His Beatitude Monsignor Michael Salah, Latin patriarch of Jerusalem, by whom we all received the order of the Pilgrim's Shell.

Lastly we went to Massada and the Dead Sea. The name of this sea is very accurate, for everything in it is dead due to its highly sulfurous waters. There are no fish, not a bird is seen to fly above it, and there are no boats. We were warned against immersing our heads, which could be fatal. I went into the water with my friend Enrique Balmes and was unlucky enough to slip and fall into the water headfirst. I struggled for a few seconds until I was able to take my head out of the water. Since I could not see a thing, Enrique had to lead me to a source of running water to wash my eyes out. A few minutes later my sight was normal, but I was left deaf and voiceless until a specialist in Madrid returned my senses to me.

We returned to Rome and stayed at the Columbus Hotel of the Vatican. Since we were to continue our travels through Europe we said good-bye to our friends who were going back to Colombia. We went to Livorno by train, and from there by boat to Barcelona where we stayed at the Presidente hotel. We saw Jaime Soto, who was the Colombian Consul at the time, and Maria Jose Cebollero, who was married to his son, the notorious Roberto Soto Prieto. We also spent time with Maria Odile and Roger Sole. Since I could neither speak nor hear, we went to Madrid where the first thing I did was see the highly recommended Doctor Velayos. After two consultations and a short treatment, I returned to normality.

In Madrid "theater of my old feats," I felt like new. I saw my "old" girlfriends; we also visited Olga Fajardo, Gloria Nannetti, Emma Villegas, and the entire Gullon de Oñate family. We had lunch with Manolo at the "Puerta de Hierro" Club and spent a day at his country home, "Santo Domingo," where we had the best paella, cooked by Jose Maria. Enrique Balmes, who was a member of the Colombian Historical Academy, brought with him some letters to the Spanish Historical Academy, which contained the names of new Academy members. Since he had to return to Colombia from Italy, he bade me represent him. I set up an appointment, and had a long interview with the director. I will never forget one of his phrases: "The happiest countries of this world are those without history."

On the eighteenth of May Pierre arrived from the

United States. One night we went with him to the great casino outside of Madrid and we won! On the twenty-fifth, day of the Argentine Independence, we attended a great reception at the Embassy. Pierre left for the French Riviera on the thirtieth, and since Lucía and I were going back to Italy, we made a date with him to meet again at the beginning of June at my cousin Augusta's home in Pavia. Meanwhile we went to France, and in Saint Jean de Luz we met with the Giraults and Charles Henri and Concha Fere once again.

After spending some wonderful days in that lovely town by the sea, we took a train that took us to Pavia. We stayed at the Moderno Hotel, and met up with Pierre, who was fascinated with Elisabetta and Alessandra, daughters of Augusta and Nadir. We went to Tromello, where my mother was born. We rented a car and on the eighth of June Pierre drove all the way to Bologna with us where one of the soccer matches of the World Cup was being held. For us this was an interesting game, for it was Colombia versus Arab Emirates, and Colombia won.

On the fifteenth of June we returned to Colombia, and Pierre to the States. We arrived on time to witness Juana's junior high school graduation at the Colegio Nueva Granada. A few days later I traveled to Atlanta with Juana, where she was to spend the rest of her summer, and from where I departed on my journey to Alaska. I went to Vancouver by plane, where I boarded the Rotterdam. Navigation lasted several days toward the north, through the isles and glaciers of the continent. Due to the warmth of summer, pieces of ice would fall from the cusps of the glaciers with tremendous crashes into the sea - truly magnificent.

The boat was especially designed for navigation on icy seas. We traveled as far north as the elements permitted. By plane, Russia could be reached in half an hour, and during the winter one can walk there through the Bering Strait. I saw Sitka, the former capital of Russia in Alaska, and Juneau, the current capital, as well as Valdez Port and Anchorage. Then in the famous train "McKinley Explorer" we headed towards Denaly National Park to observe the caribou and all sorts of animals, the Eskimos on their dog - pulled sleighs, and finally Fairbanks.

From Fairbanks I flew to San Francisco in order to attend a special dinner my children had organized for me in celebration of my forty years of marriage, on the twenty sixth of July, at the Green House Restaurant. Luis, Karen, Denise and her husband, Anna and her husband, and Jean Ehret were there, but the bride was missing.

I went to Denise's ranch in the mountains of California, and one day rode one of her motorcycles. And as they say, "A pox to old age," I fell and the bike landed on me, and miraculously I did not break one single bone. Since then, I continue to admire motorcycles, especially those modern ones that cost more than a car, although I have dedicated more time to bicycles. We said good-bye with a dinner in Karen's home, and I left for Las Vegas with Pierre. Then off to our Palm Beach apartment, where the gang from Atlanta arrived in the new van. I visited Marcial Digat in his Miami home. On August twenty third I returned to Bogotá with Juana, and the Buitrago's stayed at our apartment for a while longer.

In December, Karen came back from San Francisco and we spent that Christmas of 1990 with the "Ponchos." On the eighteenth of April of 1991, on her birthday, Karen inaugurated her art show "Pegados Mortales." Of this show art critic Miguel Gonzalez said, "Her works reveal a sentimental itinerary of dreams and desires."

Remembering the happy years we spent in New York, the place of our first home, we rented an apartment in Manhattan's Sutton Place. In May, Lucía and I started off on our trip via Cartagena and the Rosario Islands. In the capital of the world we re-visited: 57th and Lexington, 57th and Madison, and the houses we lived in with our children, on 58 Beacon Hill Road in Port Washington, and 7 France Place in Larchmont. Both are still intact because they were built the old fashioned way, with stone, bricks, and slate roofs. We saw our old neighbors and friends, who still were living around there, Signe Fay, Cecilia and Alfonso Pardo, and with them we brought many memories to mind...

We updated ourselves with Broadway, and saw the best its theaters had to offer. When IBM found out we were in New York, they sent us a limousine which took us to Armonk. We were received by the IBM Latin America group, at the time managed by Mr. Libero. We had lunch with them and then went around the beautiful facility that is surrounded by trees and fields.

We continued our trip visiting Regal Ware, business partners of Medina Hermanos, in Kewaskum, Wisconsin. We toured the great stainless steel factory, and were treated splendidly by the Regals, especially by Bill and Olive Crooker. Then off to San Francisco to visit our children. Our arrival coincided with that of Pedro and Maruja Olarte in their famous motor home. They came from Florida and it was a pleasure for us to be together again and reminisce. I had the privilege of attending their marriage in Medellin back in the forties.

We visited Denise and John in the mountains and then went to Las Vegas with Pierre. He accommodated us in the luxurious Mirage, where we were surrounded by the extravagance of the casinos and shows. We continued to Atlanta and enjoyed ourselves on Hector's boat in Lake Lanier, where Lucía showed us she was still a talented skier. When we returned to Colombia, we took Andrea with us and she had a great time with Juana, attending parties and visiting country homes with friends. On August first we celebrated Andrea's birthday with a party filled with gifts and more friends.

Anna, Pierre and Luis Jr. were present for Christmas of 1991, and together with the Medina family, we celebrated with a great turkey. On the twenty ninth, another celebration in honor of Pierre's birthday, who left together with Anna back to the States shortly thereafter.

In March 1992 Denise arrived in Colombia, and on April third, her birthday arrived with a party. Eponine was there with her theater group, who had recently participated in the International Theater Festival. With Denise we also spent a day in the great dairy farm Casablanca, which belongs to her friend Alec Gomez Sierra.

For the 1992 Olympics in Barcelona, Lucía and I departed on yet another long journey which began in June. We stayed in Concha Fere's apartment at Calle Bruc number 75 in Barcelona. She was spending the summer in St. Jean de Luz, and offered us her home. We saw the entire Olympiad, from start to finish. Concha's apartment was our base, and before and after the games we took several short trips around Spain and France to Sevilla, where we saw ExpoSevilla, Mallorca, Ibiza, Madrid, St. Jean de Luz, and Paris.

When the Olympics began, Karen came from Rome

to stay with us, and with her we saw all the games, with tickets provided to us by IBM and Coca-Cola. Those are the best Olympic games I have ever seen, well organized and with spectacular shows. When everything was over Karen left for southern Spain, we said farewell to the Soles, and on August eighth left for Atlanta. Joyce and Juana were taking a road trip from Atlanta to New York and back, and they arrived in a white convertible.

We returned to Bogotá on the twenty-eighth of August and on September fourteenth Lucía received the investiture of Lady of the Order of the Holy Sepulchre of Jerusalem. Luis Jr. returned to the States after a long while of working as editor of a Colombian television channel. For that following Christmas we received the Buitrago family and Pierre. We had many parties and gifts until 1993 came along. Everyone left on January ninth and we were left alone...

On May twenty-eighth Joyce, who had been divorced from Poncho for quite some time, married German Molano Camacho. We held a party in our home and were entertained by the "Tuna Real." On the twentieth of July, Karen arrived from Rome with a batch of fresh art produced in Italy. Vincenzo Solano came with her to attend the show she opened in the Belarca Gallery in Bogotá. The theme of the show was "Encuentros Rehechos," (Redone Encounters) and the critics said: "Artist and citizen of the world Karen Lamassonne has returned to her spiritual home with a new box of surprises." After great success with the show, Karen returned to Italy.

Juana's fifteenth birthday arrived, originating a great party in "San Alejo" in Cajica. Joyce's religious wedding ceremony took place on the eighth of December in the island of San Andres. 1993 finished with Pierre's visit and 1994 began with Karen's marriage to Gustavo Gonzalez in the Campidoglio of Rome on the fifth of February. A short while later they took up residence in Atlanta.

On May eighth I traveled to participate in the "Tour de France" bicycle race for seniors age sixty and up. The test took place in the Loire Valley during fifteen days, and I had the honor of winning the trophy. We were woken up at seven every morning, had breakfast at eight, and started pedaling at nine, rain or shine. We were twenty-five contestants, and I was the oldest one...

This was the first time in my life I went to Paris without going into Paris. I arrived from South America to the Charles de Gaulle Airport, and a car took me south on the freeway, Notre Dame in the distance. When I returned fifteen days later, I came back the same way I left, observing the same view from my window without driving into the city. From Paris I went to Atlanta where Lucía was expecting me, ready to celebrate my triumph.

Since the World Cup of soccer was taking place those days in the U.S., we rented a house in Orlando and in the Buitrago van, the whole family took off to watch the soccer games. We returned to Atlanta by way of Epcot Center, and on the twenty-first of July, an American Airlines plane took us back to Bogotá.

Gabriela, our fourth granddaughter was born on August first 1994, daughter of Joyce and German. Andrea and Gabriela now share the same birthday. Pierre and Hector took flash trips to Bogotá to meet the precious Gabriela in September. In October she was baptized with pomp and showers of gifts.

On the twenty-fourth of November Anna arrived from San Francisco with her friend Laura Stevenson. Laura is a very jolly Mormon, who after a few days of staying in our home, even received a marriage proposal! Anna had several reunions with her old friends from school, and on December twelfth I was left alone, for together with her mother, Anna went back to San Francisco. Lucía wanted to be present for the birth of our fifth granddaughter, first child of Denise and John. Her name is Veronica, and she was born on the twentieth of December. She is a precious blue eyed girl who in a few years will have the boys of neighboring towns jogging through the mountains to see her!

Since I was alone that Christmas, my good friends Ramon and Perla Meira adopted me as a member of their family and I spent the holidays with them. Lucía spent it in the cold snow at Denise's ranch, and later on went to Las Vegas with Pierre. They stayed at the MGM hotel and casino. Then together they went to Atlanta and celebrated Laura's birthday on the twenty-seventh of January and Lucía's on the fifth of February. Since Anna had switched jobs and was now living in Long Island, Lucía went to visit her and returned to Atlanta to witness the birth of Lorenzo, Karen's first son, who came into the world on April 3,1995. He is our first grandson, a beautiful baby with blond hair and blue eyes. And Karen, courageous as always, having her first baby in her forties...

The following month I went to Atlanta to meet Lorenzo, and I encountered a multitude that was there for the same reason, as if he were the Messiah. Denise, Veronica, Lucía, Juana... After offering him gold, incense, and myrrh, we said good-bye to him and dispersed in opposite directions, Denise and her daughter back to the mountains, Juana to her Trinity School in New York, and Lucía and I to Bogotá, where I had an important appointment.

My date was with Paco Barraquer, the best eye surgeon in the world. My eyes were suffering from cataracts, which impeded me from driving fast at night and made reading uncomfortable. In the United States you are not allowed to have both eyes operated at once, but Paco presented me with two options, either to operate one eye first and the other two months later, or both at once. Since I had projected a trip to Australia soon after, I said to myself: "One anesthetic, one operation," and I opted for the second choice. After the operation I remained blind and blindfolded for three days in the hospital. When the blindfold was removed I saw the world that surrounded me as when I was a boy. It was like a miracle, my pupils were removed and replaced with new ones...

Anna announced her visit a few days later, and as we were going to pick her up at the airport, a drunk driver hit our car in the back. To make the story short: policemen until dawn, our car completely destroyed, hospital, insurance check and a new car. Thank goodness this ordeal did not happen to my favorite car, an old friend of forty-one years...

As mentioned before, each year I attend the International Bonsai Convention, for it is my favorite manual pastime. In October of 1995 it took place in Australia and this time the trip was long. Bogotá, Miami, Los Angeles, Tahiti, New Zealand, where I spent several days, and finally Australia, which is a beautiful and unexplored continent. There is an abundance of land and few inhabitants. The fauna and flora are unique; the eucalyptus trees that are spread throughout the world come from Australia, and koalas and kangaroos can only be found there. The bonsai exhibitions were magnificent, created by Chinese and Japanese masters who began the technique thousands of years ago. Sydney is a marvelous city, with an opera hall of unique architecture, and its people with exemplary discipline developed by English expatriates and their descendants...

The longest flight I have ever taken in my life was from Sydney to Los Angeles: fourteen hours non-stop, but we were well taken care of since dusk, when the journey began. After the serving of appetizers, came a magnificent dinner and a good movie. Since the flight was not very full, a stewardess prepared a bed for me on four seats. I took a sleeping pill and was woken up the next morning for breakfast before landing in Los Angeles...

My return home was through San Francisco where I met up with Denise and her family. I continued to Las Vegas where I met Pierre and we dedicated our time to cleaning out the casinos. The following stop was Atlanta where I celebrated Halloween with my grandchildren. I arrived in Bogotá on November fifth, and extraordinarily enough, Lucía and I decided we would spend the holidays traveling.

We accepted an invitation to the city of Pasto in southern Colombia from Luz Estella and Lucho Chamorro. We spent Christmas with them and visited "El Santuario de las Lajas" and La Laguna de la Cocha. We received the New Year 1996 in Ecuador en route to the Galapagos Islands. We saw giant turtles, iguanas and sea lions, which you can touch while they sleep and yawn on the shore. It is unfortunate that Ecuadorians are allowing tourism to ruin this natural marvel.

The day of the Three Kings (January 6) we met Perla and Ramon Meira in Guayaquil. With them and their children: Johnny and his wife Janeth, Miguel and his wife Patricia and the grandchildren, we went to the beaches of Salinas, where they have an apartment right on the beach. We spent a few wonderful days there with them. Salinas has no reason to envy Florida's beaches, with its buildings and nautical club.

We returned to Bogotá where we met up with Pierre, who had just arrived from Peru, a bit affected by the altitude... but in the San Ignacio Hospital they cured his ailments and he was able to return to the United States. The month of April was a very busy one; on the nineteenth we celebrated Luis Jr.'s birthday, who at the time was working as a television editor. On the twenty-second, Karen, Gustavo and Lorenzo arrived and left again for Atlanta on the ninth of May. Shortly after Joyce, Gabriela, and their maid Antonia left for Spain to meet up with German in Begur (Capsasal). That summer they received Juana, Andrea, Laura, and Pierre, who took off on a journey in a rented car to Paris and London via the Chunnel, and returning through Madrid. I also arrived in the Costa Brava, invited by Joyce and German, after attending the Bonsai Convention in Washington and the Olympics in Atlanta. I returned to Bogotá at the end of the summer, passing through Saint Jean de Luz, where I saw my friends the Giraults.

A short while later, in September, Lucía traveled to San Francisco and then to Atlanta for Catalina's birth, Michele and Hector's third daughter. This precious girl "appeared" on September thirtieth. Meanwhile my grandson Lorenzo, who suffers from Hemophilia, was hospitalized in Atlanta, and a port was put in his little body to facilitate the injection of the coagulation factor that is missing in his blood.

On October twenty third I took my son Luis to the El Dorado Airport, for he was to return to San Francisco after having worked in television for a while. Luis was going back to his university studies in San Francisco, where he had two semesters remaining. And finally! -- Lucía came back to Bogotá on December fifth, after having abandoned me for so long. Joyce, German, Juana, and Gabriela came to celebrate Christmas and New Year shortly thereafter.

The Latin American Bonsai Convention of 1997 took place in Cali in March. It was lovely and I was very pleased to see my friends from the continent once again, from Argentina to the tropics. The event was presided by a great Japanese master, and organized by Solita, Cajiao, and the Botero sisters.

I also received the news of my ascension to Knight Commander of the Order of the Holy Sepulchre of Jerusalem from the Vatican in Rome.

At the end of May Lucía and I traveled to San Francisco to attend our youngest daughter Anna's wedding. She was married on the seventh of June to Maurice Conlin, an Irish gentleman. The party was magnificent: it took place in a grand room in one of the ancient palaces of the city, where apart from their local friends, the bride and groom's families came from different parts of the globe: England, Spain, and Colombia. I gave the bride away, and after the ceremony a great banquet was served to the music of the orchestra. The party finished with dancing to the beat of a Cuban band: boleros, salsa, rumba, and other rhythms.

We had a picnic at Golden Gate Park, which was reserved for the occasion, and on the grills the "chorizos" and meats smoked delightfully. There were a variety of games for children, where our small grandchildren had fun. It was the first time in twenty-one years that the entire tribe that Lucía and I founded was together...

The newlyweds went to Mexico for their honeymoon,

and Lucía and I left for Saint Louis and New Orleans. In the latter city, apart from gambling on a floating casino, we had dinner in the home of my old friends, the Martinez Mendoza sisters. The three of them live together, and the "Patoja" and I remembered the good days in Bogotá, fifty years ago, which are as dead as are our old friends of those times...

After a few days in Atlanta, we stayed at the Marriott in Miami and spent time with Milena Restrepo and her husband Ramon Quiñones and saw Marcial Digat and his daughter Mimi. We returned to Bogotá on July fourteenth. On the seventh of August we went to a party at Cristina Meira de la Espriella's home celebrating the sixtieth wedding anniversary of her parents, Perla and Ramon and their eighty-seven years of life. In September Anna came for a short visit and Estrella Arias left for Spain. Estrella was our maid for some time, and we sent her to Spain to help Joyce with Gabriela, to replace the recently departed Antonia.

In November we went on a cruise in the Caribbean with our friends Carlos and Rosalba Pacheco. We flew to Puerto Rico and visited ten islands. We navigated at night and explored the islands during the day. The ship was ten stories high, with ten elevators and all sorts of entertainment: casino, theater, swimming pool, and we played bridge with the Pacheco's every day.

We spent that Christmas in the home of Alvaro Hernan Mejia and his wife Aydee, with their children and grandchildren, since none of our own were in Colombia. In February our house was active and full of joy once again with Karen and Joyce's arrivals. They had Lorenzo and Gabriela with them, who showed their love for each other by playing and fighting all the time.

On April twenty-third I left for El Paso, Texas, to meet with Manuel Gullon de Oñate (Manolo), who arrived from Madrid with his niece Blanca Meza de Oñate. This was an invitation from the Governor of Texas, George W. Bush, son of the former President of the United States, to celebrate the fourth centennial of Don Juan Oñate's entrance to Texas. Manolo is a descendant of Don Juan Oñate, who colonized Texas, New Mexico and Arizona, and introduced the first horse to the United States. Since the Prince of Spain was unable to attend the festivities, the Vice President, Don Francisco Alvarez-Cascos, came accompanied by soldiers of the Iberian Peninsula, who marched in the same attire that was used four-hundred years ago. Since Manolo was the guest of honor, he was kept quite busy all the time with banquets, masses, and parades.

I took a day to celebrate on my own. From my hotel I walked from the United States to Mexico. I crossed the Rio Grande through the same place Don Juan did four centuries ago, with the difference that today there is a bridge which marks the border between the two countries. I wasn't asked for my documents to enter the city of Juarez, to which I arrived after a two-hour walk. I spent the greater part of my day in Mexico, walking around and eating enchiladas. I returned on foot, but this time I was asked for identification. Thank goodness I had my passport...

The celebration continued in New Mexico with indigenous tribes, and later in Santa Fe, where Governor Johnson was our host. We stayed at the "El Dorado" Hotel in this beautiful city, which, in the preservation of its tradition, does not even have a commercial airport. Airplanes arrive in Albuquerque and then one must travel one hundred kilometers (62 miles) by car. The festivities in Santa Fe surpassed all the previous ones: a solemn mass in the cathedral, speeches and parading of soldiers on foot and horseback, and a great luncheon presided by Governor Johnson in the "Las Golondrinas" Museum. In a grand act of the National Guard, Manolo had to uncover the statue of "Don Juan." Blanca and I were driven by no less than Senator Tom Benavides, who took us everywhere in his car, including the Senate building, where he has occupied his seat for the last twenty-five years...

Once the festivities were over, I invited Manolo to travel with me to Atlanta and spend a few days in the home of my daughter Michele, whom he has known since she was a little girl. Due to prior engagements, he was unable to accompany me. It was a shame, because my son-in-law Gustavo Gonzalez and I had prepared an interview on Spanish CNN for him.

I came to Atlanta alone, and I can now give myself the pleasure of turning from past times to the present. I am no longer sitting at home in front of my "IBM Aptiva," but in front of another, (which name I do not wish to recall, in order to not advertise the competition) which belongs to my son-in-law Hector.

In this beautiful city, Atlanta, which grows day and night, (especially at night when the politicians are asleep,) is where I have the greatest number of family members: my daughter Michele, her husband Hector Buitrago, and their three daughters Andrea, Laura, and Catalina. My daughter Karen, her husband Gustavo, and their son Lorenzo live nearby. Their homes are outside of the city, surrounded by trees and forests, where you can breathe fresh air.

I just spoke to Lucía, who traveled from Colombia to California a few days ago, to visit the part of the family that lives there: our daughter Denise, her husband John Ehret, and their daughter Veronica, who live on a ranch in the mountains surrounded by many acres of land and trees; our daughter Anna and her husband Maurice Conlin, who live in an apartment in San Francisco; our son Pierre, who lives in Reno; and lastly (and I've left him for last for a very special reason) our son Luis, who will receive his diploma at San Francisco State University tomorrow...

I spoke with Lucía and Luis, and tomorrow, together with the other members of my family who are there, she will attend the graduation ceremonies and together they will all celebrate the event. Although far, I will be with them in spirit. They told me San Francisco is cold today, while here the air is wonderfully warm. At noon we went to mass at a nearby parochial church. The name of the church is Transfiguration, and the priest is Father Patrick Bishop. The service lasts an hour and a half, and it is the most unique I have seen in my life for its hymns, music, and the instruments used. For communion, numerous jars of wine and loaves of bread, which are broken into small pieces, are taken to the altar. Those of us who take communion, we eat that bread and have a sip of that wine...

Lucía and I will be reunited next week, and we will stay here a long time because Michele and Hector are going to Europe to see the World Cup very soon. They will be rooting for the Colombian team, which has classified for this great event. The matches will take place all over France, the final being in Paris. In the meantime, we will stay here as parents and grandparents to Andrea, Laura, and Catalina. Speaking of which, this weekend we visited Andrea at her university in Athens. She is studying in that great school with a full scholarship, awarded to her for being a brilliant high school student. As the saying goes, "like mother, like daughter."

In this neighborhood we are surrounded by a Colombian colony so devoted to soccer, that a small league of aficionados has formed. They play every weekend and have their own set of rules, for the teams are comprised of both men and women, and when a woman scores a goal, it counts for two. The games are played in fields that belong to Cobb County. Michele and Hector are avid participants, mainly for the exercise, as are most of the other participating couples.

After each game, they celebrate with a get-together in one of their homes, where each person takes his own share of food, drink, or dessert. Children and friends are invited to the games as well as the aftermath. I have been to several of the games and parties at the homes of Jorge and Helena Simmonds, Fabrizio and Jeffrey Tapia, Ricardo and Paulette Moncada, Gustavo and Marta Duran, Alvaro and Jane Lievano, Jim and Olivia O'Shea, Jim and Maria Lankford, Joe and Diana Pair, Don and Nancy Nason, Jan and Debbie Russell, Ivan and Estela Bilbao, and others who escape me at the moment.

CHAPTER 10

EPILOGUE

IBM - FROM THE OUTSIDE LOOKING IN

It's 1998 and I'm now 88 years old. I started out in IBM in 1933 and left after 38 years of employment, so I'm probably the oldest existing IBM retiree, considering the date of my initiation.

During these last 26 years I've lived a second life, spending all my time on what I liked best. But I never lost sight of IBM and from the outside I was able to observe it wholeheartedly as something mine, affectionately and with a critical sense. This is only logical because after my retirement in 1972, I felt I was part owner of the company since, together with my salary, I received stocks and dividends.

Just as it had been foreseen, Frank Cary took charge of IBM in 1973. Even though the lawsuit for a monopoly continued, the company kept growing at a tremendous pace.

Although it wasn't public knowledge, the company was preparing for the possibility that it be divided in several parts, as had occurred in the past with other big companies. Frank Cary's assistant, John Opel, was his right-hand man and was the person he was grooming to succeed him when the time came for his retirement. I knew John well, since he was a member of our 1062 sales school in Endicott in 1950, when he was starting his career with IBM.

The era of the System 370 had started and it sold like hot cakes, with other new systems, such as the 3033, the 4300, the 32 and the 34. Sales were easier and easier to realize day after day. In one of my many trips to the U.S., as a mere coincidence, I was in an IBM office and I heard how a salesman was taking an order over the phone for a system that was worth over a million dollars! This to me was unheard of. During my time as a salesman, a sale of that nature was done in a ceremonious way in the office of our customer, with the signing of the contract, after studying the customer's needs over a long period of time.

I was so disappointed by seeing this drastic change in our way of selling, that I immediately started to sell a part of the IBM stock that I had, which was worth 500 dollars per share. This, compounded with the bureaucracy that continued to grow without limits, made me see a cloudy future for the company...

In 1981 IBM launched the personal computer, which at first was considered of little importance - it was even launched with a Charles Chaplin theme, and it represented only a small percentage of the company's profits. We never thought that this business would carry the importance that it does today, causing a computer revolution around the world, with many new competitors, which took a lead on IBM, particularly in the area of programming. Bill Gates and his leading software company, Microsoft, was considering working and collaborating for IBM when he first started. This young man never in his wildest dreams imagined that he would be the mogul that he is today, facing Uncle Sam in a monopoly lawsuit. This is the sin that large companies fall in, just like what happened to IBM.

And while I'm in the topic of monopolies, in January

1982, after 13 years of a long-drawn court battle, the U.S. government decided to dismiss the case against IBM due to lack of merits! I think it was a fair verdict, since during all those years, many competitors sprang up with new products. It was the longest monopoly law suit in history and it was the only one that the government didn't win, except the case in 1920 against U.S. Steel that lasted 9 years. The previous monopoly law suits that took place were: in 1911 against Standard Oil that lasted 5 years; in 1911 against American Tobacco that also latest 5 years; in 1945 against Aluminum Co. of America that lasted 8 years; in 1948 against Paramount Pictures that lasted 10 years and in 1982 against AT&T that dragged on for 8 years.

As planned, in 1983 John Opel became the big boss in IBM. I remember him from back in 1950 when he was a young student in our 1062 sales school in Endicott. During two months, I would observe those students that excelled and he stood out from all the others in our all-day classes. By his intelligent questions and participation, I could tell that John would go far in his career with IBM, and that happened 33 years later.

Not only did bureaucracy grow in IBM, but so did the arrogance of the Company amidst its grandeur. The sun never set in the IBM Empire. It had more than 400,000 employees worldwide, and its net profits were the largest that any company had ever achieved. In the meantime, the most important things that existed when I worked in IBM were disappearing: the "marriage" with our customers, the leasing of equipment, salesman that were solely IBM, the best service, our human relations, our open-door policy and our IBM family...

John Opel tried to restore those virtues that IBM had

lost and that had once been preached in IBM's sales school as the golden rule back in 1950. But time caught up with him. His retirement came along and he handed it all over to John Akers in 1986.

Some say that John Akers was a good salesman, but as President and Chairman of the Board of IBM he was disastrous. During his years in power, IBM took one step ahead and two steps backwards. He was arrogant and fired personnel left and right without caring about the company's policy. Since IBM never had a union, the group "United Employees of IBM" was formed and despised him and wrote verses in which Akers was depicted as a false man and as a villain...

What happened was bound to happen. A good organization could not be directed with just the help of bureaucratic pals, but it also needed the collaboration of all the employees. The best people abandoned the company and took with them in their brains the company's secrets to other places where they would be treated better. Sales declined as well as the company's profits and the value of its stock took a tumble too.

In 1989 and 1990 Akers committed another fatal error. In order to stop IBM's stock from going down and to inspire confidence with the investment community, he ordered IBM to buy back its own shares at an average of $119 per share. In that sole operation, IBM lost 3.5 billion dollars because each share went down to less than 50 dollars. It was a total catastrophe; in 1990 IBM's net profit was six billion dollars; whereas in 1992, it's net loss was of five billion! The total value of its shares went down 75 billion dollars and for the first time in its history, IBM lowered its dividends by 1.5 billion dollars a year!

John Akers, the man who never took no for an answer,

finally resigned after so much pressure and embarrassment. For the first time in the history of IBM, the board of directors assumed the task of finding someone to fill this position from outside of the company. Someone without commitments and buddies and favorites within the organization, that could get it back on track...

In early 1993 they found my namesake, Louis V. Gerstner, who had rescued Nabisco and American Express out of the "abyss". He was 54 and had no idea about computers, but as a good business consultant, he possessed a special sense to do what was right at the right moment. He removed all the bureaucratic "dead wood" from IBM and brought in some experts that he knew. Some tightening up had to be done, and in his first year he fired 60,000 employees!

The results speak for themselves. In 1994, after three consecutive years of big losses, IBM made a comeback, posting net after-tax income in 1995 of 4.1 billion dollars, in 1996 of 5.4 billion and in 1997 of over 6 billion dollars.

I haven't met Lou Gerstner personally, but I would like to congratulate him on this economic miracle he achieved in such a short period of time. And now that IBM is doing well economically, I would ask him if in the future he plans to renew all those things that were once so important for the company and were lost through time, such as the annual reunions of The Quarter Century Club and the real open door policy and human relations that were once part of my life with IBM...

ABOUT THE AUTHOR

Luis A. Lamassonne was born in La Plata, Argentina on March 6, 1910. He studied journalism in the University of La Plata and he has coursed other studies in England, Scotland and the United States.

He has enriched his life with extracurricular activities such as the Presidency of the Colombian American Chamber of Commerce in Bogotá, Colombia; the Presidency of the Colombian American Chamber of Commerce in New York, where he was reelected six times; member of the board of directors of Incolda and Diriventas and of the board of directors of the Rotary Club of Bogotá and Medellin. He received the high honor from the President of the Republic of Colombia of the Order of San Carlos, in appreciation for services rendered to the country. Many other organizations in the areas of philanthropy, education, business and social development have been enriched by this man both in Colombia and in the United States.

Sensitive to the arts and a lover of life, nature, and one of his most passionate activities, the art of Bonsai.

In October 2000, at the age of ninety years, he moved from Bogota, Colombia to the city of Miami, where he currently lives with his wife Lucía.

Jose D. Buitrago M.